Online Resources

You now have access to practical templates and case studies for the Business Ethics concepts covered in this book. These downloadable resources offer guidance for developing and implementing ethical practices in business operations, giving you an in-depth understanding of key concepts.

These resources, as listed below, include five essential templates:

- Ethical Decision-Making Template
- Code of Ethics Template
- Stakeholder Engagement Sample Strategy
- Ethics Training Program Sample Outline
- Impact Assessment Strategy Template

To access the templates, follow the steps below:

1. Scan the QR code below to land on the product page.
2. Request the online resources by filling in the required details.

Happy self-learning!

bit.ly/be-slm

This page is intentionally left blank

SELF-LEARNING MANAGEMENT SERIES

VIBRANT
PUBLISHERS™

BUSINESS ETHICS ESSENTIALS

YOU ALWAYS WANTED TO KNOW

Your Valuable Companion in Solving
Ethical Business Dilemmas

DR. RITIKA MAHAJAN

BUSINESS ETHICS ESSENTIALS YOU ALWAYS WANTED TO KNOW

First Edition

© 2025, By Vibrant Publishers, USA. All rights reserved. No part of this publication may be reproduced or distributed in any form or by any means, or stored in a database or retrieval system, without the prior permission of the publisher.

Paperback ISBN 10: 1-63651-332-8
Paperback ISBN 13: 978-1-63651-332-4

Ebook ISBN 10: 1-63651-333-6
Ebook ISBN 13: 978-1-63651-333-1

Hardback ISBN 10: 1-63651-334-4
Hardback ISBN 13: 978-1-63651-334-8

Library of Congress Control Number: 2024949781

Vibrant Publishers books are available at special quantity discount for sales promotions, or for use in corporate training programs. For more information please write to bulkorders@vibrantpublishers.com

Please email feedback / corrections (technical, grammatical or spelling) to spellerrors@vibrantpublishers.com

To access the complete catalogue of Vibrant Publishers, visit www.vibrantpublishers.com

V1.1-325

SELF-LEARNING MANAGEMENT SERIES

TITLE	PAPERBACK* ISBN
BUSINESS AND ENTREPRENEURSHIP	
BUSINESS COMMUNICATION ESSENTIALS	9781636511634
BUSINESS ETHICS ESSENTIALS	9781636513324
BUSINESS INTELLIGENCE ESSENTIALS	9781636513362
BUSINESS LAW ESSENTIALS	9781636511702
BUSINESS PLAN ESSENTIALS	9781636511214
BUSINESS STRATEGY ESSENTIALS	9781949395778
ENTREPRENEURSHIP ESSENTIALS	9781636511603
INTERNATIONAL BUSINESS ESSENTIALS	9781636513294
PRINCIPLES OF MANAGEMENT ESSENTIALS	9781636511542
COMPUTER SCIENCE AND TECHNOLOGY	
BLOCKCHAIN ESSENTIALS	9781636513003
MACHINE LEARNING ESSENTIALS	9781636513775
PYTHON ESSENTIALS	9781636512938
DATA SCIENCE FOR BUSINESS	
DATA ANALYTICS ESSENTIALS	9781636511184
FINANCIAL LITERACY AND ECONOMICS	
COST ACCOUNTING & MANAGEMENT ESSENTIALS	9781636511030
FINANCIAL ACCOUNTING ESSENTIALS	9781636510972
FINANCIAL MANAGEMENT ESSENTIALS	9781636511009
MACROECONOMICS ESSENTIALS	9781636511818
MICROECONOMICS ESSENTIALS	9781636511153
PERSONAL FINANCE ESSENTIALS	9781636511849

*Also available in Hardback & Ebook formats

SELF-LEARNING MANAGEMENT SERIES

TITLE	PAPERBACK* ISBN

HUMAN RESOURCE AND ORGANIZATIONAL SUCCESS

DIVERSITY, EQUITY, AND INCLUSION ESSENTIALS	9781636512976
DIVERSITY IN THE WORKPLACE ESSENTIALS	9781636511122
HR ANALYTICS ESSENTIALS	9781636510347
HUMAN RESOURCE MANAGEMENT ESSENTIALS	9781949395839
ORGANIZATIONAL BEHAVIOR ESSENTIALS	9781636512303
ORGANIZATIONAL DEVELOPMENT ESSENTIALS	9781636511481

LEADERSHIP AND PERSONAL DEVELOPMENT

DECISION MAKING ESSENTIALS	9781636510026
INDIA'S ROAD TO TRANSFORMATION: WHY LEADERSHIP MATTERS	9781636512273
LEADERSHIP ESSENTIALS	9781636510316
TIME MANAGEMENT ESSENTIALS	9781636511665

MODERN MARKETING AND SALES

CONSUMER BEHAVIOR ESSENTIALS	9781636513263
DIGITAL MARKETING ESSENTIALS	9781949395747
MARKETING MANAGEMENT ESSENTIALS	9781636511788
MARKET RESEARCH ESSENTIALS	9781636513744
SALES MANAGEMENT ESSENTIALS	9781636510743
SERVICES MARKETING ESSENTIALS	9781636511733
SOCIAL MEDIA MARKETING ESSENTIALS	9781636512181

*Also available in Hardback & Ebook formats

SELF-LEARNING MANAGEMENT SERIES

TITLE	PAPERBACK* ISBN
OPERATIONS AND PROJECT MANAGEMENT	
AGILE ESSENTIALS	9781636510057
OPERATIONS & SUPPLY CHAIN MANAGEMENT ESSENTIALS	9781949395242
PROJECT MANAGEMENT ESSENTIALS	9781636510712
STAKEHOLDER ENGAGEMENT ESSENTIALS	9781636511511

CURRENT AFFAIRS

DIGITAL SHOCK	9781636513805

*Also available in Hardback & Ebook formats

This page is intentionally left blank

About the Author

Dr. Ritika Mahajan is a distinguished academician and consultant. She currently serves as a faculty member in General Management and Strategy at the Department of Management Studies, Malaviya National Institute of Technology (MNIT) Jaipur. A UGC-sponsored fellow, she holds a PhD degree from the prestigious Indian Institute of Technology (IIT) Roorkee, where her insightful research was published as a book.

An accomplished educator, Dr. Mahajan has held visiting faculty positions at esteemed institutions such as IIIT Lucknow, TERI School of Advanced Studies, Shiv Nadar University, and the University of Delhi. Additionally, she has coordinated the Master of Business Administration (MBA) program in Sustainability Management at TERI School of Advanced Studies previously, showcasing her commitment to fostering future leaders in sustainable business practices.

In consultancy roles, Dr. Mahajan has worked with the United Nations Environment Program (UNEP) and the Ministry of MSME, Government of India, reflecting her impact on national and international policy. With more than 50 research papers, book chapters and articles published, she is a prolific contributor to her field. She has also co-authored two scholarly books, "Business Economics and Sustainable Development: The Emerging Issues" and "Management Education in India: Masters Speak" previously. Additionally, she has delivered more than 50 sessions at both national and international programs. She teaches courses focused on strategy, communication, and ethics, and is passionate about mentoring students in business, management, and life.

Her expertise has also been sought as a visiting trainer at the Indian Institute of Coal Management and the Rajasthan Police Academy. As the Coordinator of Wellness, reporting to the Dean of Student Welfare, Dr. Mahajan actively champions mental health awareness on campus, underscoring her holistic approach to education.

What experts say about this book!

"*Business Ethics Essentials*" by Dr. Ritika Mahajan is a much-needed and timely guide for anyone navigating the complex world of ethical decision-making in business. What makes this book stand out is its ability to balance theories with real-world applications—making it both insightful and practical.

Dr. Mahajan weaves together critical topics like sustainability, corporate governance, and responsible leadership in a way that is clear, compelling, and highly relevant to today's business landscape. Whether you're a student, educator, or business leader, this book offers valuable perspectives and actionable insights to build a strong ethical foundation.

– Professor Jagdish N. Sheth, Kellstadt Professor of Business Emory University, Recipient of Padma Bhushan Award (2020)

This book provides a clear, structured introduction to business ethics, offering practical guidance for professionals at all levels—not just those in legal or HR roles. It's equally valuable for executives and business students. The chapter on marketing and advertising, for instance, demonstrates the book's broad applicability.

Each chapter features thought-provoking discussion questions and quizzes to reinforce learning.

Overall, I highly recommend this book to anyone looking for a thorough and methodical exploration of business ethics.

– Donald Farmer, Principal, TreeHive Strategy

What experts say about this book!

Dr. Ritika Mahajan's *Business Ethics Essentials* offers a masterful examination of ethical dilemmas across the full range of business functions. What distinguishes this work is its seamless integration of philosophical depth with managerial practicality.

With rare skill, Dr. Mahajan encourages readers to grapple with abstract ethical principles while keeping their focus firmly on real-world applications. The book inspires reflective thought while providing clear, actionable guidance—equally illuminating for scholars and practitioners. Aptly titled, Business Ethics Essentials proves itself indispensable to anyone engaged in the study or practice of ethical business leadership.

– Rajat Panwar, Professor of Responsible and Sustainable Business, Oregon State University, USA

This book is one that's long waited for. Ethics is something too relative and abstract, particularly when it's considered in managing business.

"*Business Ethics Essentials*" quite skilfully provides a tangible and feasible framework for practitioners. Very well organized, indeed. Language is crisp and clear. References are authentic. One can easily start applying practical ethics with the ultimate objective of getting motivated for a transcendental transition.

– Professor Manipadma Datta, PhD, FCS, GCPCL, Former Vice Chancellor, TERI School of Advanced Studies (TERI SAS), New Delhi, India

What experts say about this book!

"Business Ethics Essentials You Always Wanted to Know" by Dr. Ritika Mahajan is an indispensable guide for navigating the often complex world of ethical decision-making in business.

This book excels in presenting foundational theories, practical frameworks, and real-world examples, making it a valuable resource for professionals, educators, and students alike. Dr. Mahajan's ability to seamlessly integrate sustainability, corporate responsibility, and governance into the broader discourse of business ethics is commendable.

Whether you're grappling with ethical dilemmas or striving to foster an ethical corporate culture, this book offers clear, actionable insights for achieving integrity and accountability in today's fast-evolving business landscape. A must-read for anyone committed to ethical leadership!

– Rajesh Ranjan, MS,
Carnegie Mellon University, USA

Business Ethics Essentials is a practical and insightful guide. Dr. Mahajan does a great job combining theories, real-life examples, and practical tips. The book covers important topics like sustainability, leadership, and corporate governance in a way that's easy to understand. It's a valuable read for anyone looking to build an ethical and successful business. Clear, thoughtful, and highly relevant.

– Vaibhav Aggarwal, Doctoral Researcher,
United Nations University-Flores, Germany

What experts say about this book!

This book, *Business Ethics Essentials*, by Dr. Ritika Mahajan is a remarkable addition to the library of knowledge relating to this complex subject. This topic is very relevant, especially in this changing world, where it is extremely important to ethically carry out business in an increasingly globalized world. The treatment is very systematic and the author covers the topics starting from fundamentals to applications with the right level of detail.

After reading this book, the reader will certainly get a practical level of expertise on this subject. The heart of the book, covering sustainability, ethical business practices, leadership and corporate governance, is an eye-opener, and should be a must-read for all business leaders. The author should be congratulated on a wonderful achievement.

– Dr. Prankul Middha, Operations Director at Lightbeam.ai
BTech (IIT-D), MSc (Univ of Delaware, USA), PhD (Univ of Bergen, Norway)

"Dr. Ritika Mahajan's *Business Ethics Essentials You Always Wanted to Know* is a well-structured introduction to ethical decision-making in business. One of its strengths is its clarity—complex concepts like deontology and utilitarianism are explained in an accessible manner.

The inclusion of case studies, discussion questions, and quizzes makes it an interactive learning resource. The chapters on ethical challenges in marketing, HR, and finance offer valuable real-world applications. Overall, it's a solid foundational book on business ethics. If you're looking for a structured, educational approach to ethical decision-making, this is a great resource."

– Rishi Raman, Founder and Consulting Editor,
Indian HR Associates

What experts say about this book!

"*Business Ethics Essentials*" addresses a broad array of topics—from finance to human resources and more. I particularly appreciate how the initial sections provide a solid theoretical foundation for these subjects, offering valuable context and framing. Overall, the language used is clear, well-structured, and easy to follow, making the book a helpful overview for different categories of readers, including professionals, students, and practitioners in various fields.

Overall, this book tackles a timely and essential topic, exploring business ethics in these turbulent times at the intersection of social, technological, and economic forces. It offers clear, practical insights for anyone seeking to navigate the rapidly evolving corporate landscape while building on ethical integrity—a must-read in today's business world.

– Prof. Filippo Marchesani, Professor of "Management of Innovation" and "Digital Consumer Behavior", Department of Management and Business Administration, University "G. d'Annunzio" Chieti-Pescara

"*Business Ethics Essentials*" gives major insights into solving ethical dilemmas in our day-to-day business dealings across various areas like marketing, human resources, and finance. It talks about the ethical dilemmas businesses face and also gives an idea of what can be done in such situations. The flow is smooth, covering all important topics in business ethics. The book moves logically from understanding ethics to applying it in different business areas and then looking at future challenges.

It's written in a simple, conversational way that's easy to follow. The explanations don't feel heavy or overly academic, which makes the book engaging. The author really knows the art of writing—her words flow naturally. The book challenges readers to think deeply about ethical dilemmas rather than just providing surface-level explanations. It's a valuable guide for anyone looking to navigate the grey areas of business with confidence and clarity.

– Professor Vinay Sharma,
Department of Management Studies, Indian Institute of Technology (IIT) Roorkee

This page is intentionally left blank

Table of Contents

Acknowledgments

I would like to acknowledge the support from Vibrant Publishers, especially from their marketing and editorial teams, who answered all my queries promptly and created an incredible work environment. I am thankful to the editorial team for patiently reviewing my writing and enriching it with a keen sense of observation. I am also thankful to my students, Shubhangi and Kratika, who, with a lot of reverence and genuine hard work, helped in compiling all the references and resources.

As I near the completion of this book, I find myself stepping back to reflect on what has been created. The final outcome—a printed book—may carry the name of one person, or a few in the case of co-authors. However, no creation, no matter how small, is ever truly the work of a single individual. Every creation is the culmination of the author's knowledge, emotions, and experiences, shaped by countless contributions from many people over time.

For me, these people include my family, friends, teachers, colleagues, and students—those who have influenced and molded me, enabling me to achieve my lifelong dream of becoming an author.

This is only the beginning...

This page is intentionally left blank

Preface

As we have progressed economically, the toll on our social and environmental landscapes has become clear. Technical progress has come at the cost of air and water quality, affecting our basic necessities, especially for the economically disadvantaged. Real progress requires sustainable growth that balances our economic, social, and ecological outcomes. This kind of progress must be free from environmental degradation and the worsening of social inequality. For this, we must nurture businesses that internalize ethics in their vision, mission, objectives, core business models, and day-to-day decision-making.

As an instructor, I often encounter questions like: "How can one teach ethics?," "Shouldn't ethics be part of primary education?," "Aren't ethics personal?," "How can we decide what is right and wrong for everybody?," "Isn't the law enough?" Still, I feel strongly aligned with the need to resolve these questions and present a complete insight into business ethics.

This book aims to bring together all the theoretical, foundational, and practical information needed to run an ethical business that supports sustainable development. It offers insights into the role of ethics across various business functions. It shall serve anyone who wishes to understand business ethics, question its relevance, explore its implementation, judge business dilemmas through an ethical lens, or has related practical or fundamental questions. It also presents ways to address ethical challenges in business.

While I agree that it is not easy to navigate business ethics— given that ethical options often seem confusing or overlapping in different contexts—I believe that not accepting ethics in a business context will do more harm than good, as we are already experiencing. Supporting ethics rather than discarding them is essential for creating a better world for future generations.

Although I've authored a book on business ethics, I envision a future where it becomes part of everyday life for individuals and businesses alike, rather than being seen as a standalone subject. With warmth and determination, I have drawn on all my experience and knowledge to create **Business Ethics Essentials You Always Wanted to Know (Business Ethics Essentials)**, and I'm thrilled to see it realized through the support of my dedicated publisher.

Introduction to the book

Today, the world faces numerous challenges stemming from environmental degradation, including climate change, biodiversity loss, natural disasters, and deforestation—each of which hinders sustainable development. Additionally, human greed and aggression have led to financial fraud and mismanagement, causing recurring economic and social crises.

The path forward is to promote and support businesses that prioritize both people and the planet while maintaining profitability. As one of the most influential forces in society, businesses have a profound impact on people's lives, making ethics central to responsible business practices.

In a world increasingly aware of the impacts of corporate actions, business ethics have become indispensable for sustainable growth. As businesses navigate the complex, interconnected challenges of the 21st century—such as global inequality and the rapid rise of digital technologies—ethics provide the compass for ensuring that organizations operate with integrity, transparency, and accountability.

However, it is easier said than done. While it is clear that to save the world for our future generations, we rely on the power of ethical businesses, there are dilemmas in meeting the conflicting needs of stakeholders in an ethical company.

The book Business Ethics Essentials is an attempt to provide a complete guide to the concepts and practices of Business Ethics. It covers the origin and evolution of ethics, theories and frameworks, conceptual and practical examples, along with case studies. It is appropriate for entrepreneurs, leaders, professionals, and other stakeholders who wish to dive deep into the domain of business ethics.

The book is structured broadly into four parts. Part I covers meaning, significance, theories, and frameworks of business ethics. Part II seeks to explain contemporary ideas like CSR, sustainability, and corporate governance and how they relate to ethics. Part III covers ethical issues and cases across management functions, including finance, human resource management, marketing, and advertising. The book ends with an insight into trends, challenges, and opportunities. By the end of this book, the readers shall be able to:

- Gain comprehensive knowledge about the origin and evolution of business ethics
- Distinguish between different philosophies and theories on business ethics
- Empathize with people belonging to different schools of thought
- Learn about universal tests to make ethical decisions
- Propose frameworks for business organizations to implement and internalize ethics
- Reflect and resolve ethical dilemmas across functional areas of management
- Appreciate and adapt to challenges and opportunities emerging in this domain

How to use this book?

Business Ethics Essentials is divided into ten chapters, broadly categorized into four parts. Although each part covers independent topics, reading the book sequentially would be beneficial. The content is designed to guide the reader from retrospective analysis to forward-looking perspectives.

The first part covers conceptual understanding of ethics, origin and evolution, theories, and frameworks for ethical decision-making. The chapters in this section aim to enable the reader to understand diverse philosophies. These chapters should be read with a critical but open mind, willing to accept different viewpoints. In addition to history and theories, the tests and frameworks provide insight into decision-making based on these viewpoints.

As we move forward, part two discusses both traditional and emerging topics like CSR, sustainability, and corporate governance, and how they relate to business ethics. An understanding of these concepts is crucial to progress through the book, as one becomes acquainted with diverse terminology, contemporary trends, issues, and challenges. Leadership for running an ethical business is also explained in detail in this part.

As one progresses to part three, examples and cases from different management areas, such as finance, marketing, advertising, and human resource management are introduced. The chapters in this part provide exposure to cases of ethical dilemmas in various management functions and offer solutions from an ethical perspective. The final segment of the book addresses new trends, challenges, and opportunities, preparing the reader to imagine what the future of business ethics holds. The best outcome from this book will emerge if one reads it with a mindset that embraces the power of doing well by doing good—because, in the end, there is no better way forward!

Who can benefit from this book?

Anyone seeking to understand ethics in a business context and looking for a detailed reference will benefit from Business Ethics Essentials. Specifically, this book is valuable for:

- Industry professionals and leaders keen on exploring a comprehensive resource on business ethics
- Entrepreneurs looking to navigate ethical dilemmas and enhance decision-making
- Researchers intending to gain an in-depth insight into the field of business ethics
- Academicians looking for a text or reference book for a course on business ethics
- Students willing to understand the conceptual and practical aspects of business ethics

This page is intentionally left blank

Chapter 1

Introduction to Business Ethics

KEY LEARNING OBJECTIVES

- Define the meaning of business ethics.
- Explain the need for business ethics.
- Distinguish between ethics, morals, and values.
- Demonstrate the concept of an ethical company.
- Discuss why ethics are essential in a "company" form of business organization.

This chapter offers an introduction to the concept of business ethics. We delve into the conceptual understanding of "business ethics." We explain how and why ethics matter in the business context. The sub-sections include the meaning and need for business ethics. We also explore the differences between ethics, morals, and values that can enable one to make business decisions with clarity of thought.

Given the abstractness of the concept of business ethics, we will attempt to clarify the meaning of an ethical company. An ethical company can be described from both a positive and negative lens. In the concluding section, we shed light on the criticality of ethics for running a business.

The chapter aims to provide a strong conceptual foundation for understanding business ethics. Ethics are vital for providing a framework for decision-making in businesses, specifically companies. This is because decisions made in these organizations affect multiple stakeholders' interests.

1.1 Understanding Business Ethics

The term "Business Ethics" includes two words: business and ethics. As an activity, business refers to the buying and selling of goods and services by an individual or an organization with profit as the key motive. A business entity utilizes society's resources to generate a return on investment or, in other words - wealth.

This is a business' prime focus; ancillary objectives may include providing employment opportunities, fulfilling unmet needs, and creating a brand. They may also include market development, expansion through integration or diversification, undertaking corporate social responsibility (CSR) activities, philanthropy, etc. The latter word, i.e. ethics, can be explained as norms and standards based on society's beliefs. Ethics are expected to be followed uniformly by people living in that society. In a specific context, "right" and "wrong" related to any decision are evaluated in line with these beliefs.

These beliefs are held by a majority of the people in that context. This means a business operating in that context must abide by those beliefs. Ethics may overlap with legal requirements, but in certain instances, ethics contradict laws.

Combining the two, business ethics refers to the "code of conduct," to be followed by businesses in their commercial activities within societies. It is essential to meet such expectations, to make the firm appear ethical in the eyes of the people, for whom the business survives and thrives.

There are many forms of business organizations on a spectrum ranging from small-scale sole proprietors to large multinational corporations. As we move from one end of the spectrum to another, and as organizations grow, the complexity of management increases. With this, the need to acknowledge and address ethical concerns becomes more important.

1.1.1 Historical context of business ethics

As a discipline, business ethics is a relatively new body of knowledge in the business and management domain. It started gaining significance, particularly after the revelation of financial frauds by giant multinational corporations, global banks, and high net-worth individuals and the 2008 subprime crisis leading to the Great Recession.[1]

However, the ideation, existence, relevance, and prevalence of business ethics are as old as the concept of business itself. For example, values related to employee care and empathy, conservation of biodiversity, or transforming community lives are not new discoveries. Many businesses have integrated these values and actions into their mission, vision, objectives, code of conduct, and operations since the time they have existed in the market.

Besides financial fraud and challenges, global and national concerns for society and the environment have also increased stakeholder awareness and the emphasis on business ethics. Such concerns have been spearheaded in the last three decades. In 1987, the World Commission for Sustainable Development released the "Brundtland Commission Report." This report defined and explained sustainable development as "development that meets

---

1. M.K. Brunnermeier, "Deciphering the Liquidity and Credit Crunch 2007-2008," *Journal of Economic Perspectives* 23, no. 1 (2009): 77-100, https://doi.org/10.1257/jep.23.1.774o

the needs of the present, without compromising the ability of future generations to meet their own needs."[2]

The following decades witnessed governments formulating policies for businesses to consider social and environmental impacts. These policies aimed to ensure that economic decisions contribute to the overarching, macro-level goal of sustainable development. Together, the nations committed to the Sustainable Development Goals (SDGs) by 2030. The SDGs are a set of 17 goals and 169 targets to achieve peace and prosperity for people and the planet.[3]

Thus, business ethics gained importance because of the contemporary policy debate on the need to protect society and the environment for future generations.

Against this backdrop, this book is a complete, essential guide to the concept and discipline of business ethics. It is written to share comprehensive yet simply presented knowledge on business ethics, with a global audience. It covers the fundamentals of business ethics including the need, meaning, and significance with relevant examples and cases. It discusses different theories and perspectives related to business ethics.

Further, it proposes the structure and frameworks for ethical decision-making while discussing popularly used tests for evaluating ethical choices. These tests are based on different methods and perspectives to evaluate business dilemmas and make the right decisions. The book also provides practical insight by discussing ethical issues and concerns across different specializations in business and management such as marketing, finance, human resource (HR) management, and strategy.

Evidence from across the globe, international and national perspectives, emerging challenges, and opportunities are also included. Finally, it presents the role of leadership and corporate

---

2. "Brundtland Commission Report," World Commission for Sustainable Development, accessed July 12, 2024, https://sustainabledevelopment.un.org

3. "Sustainable Development Goals (SDGs) (Agenda 2030)," United Nations, accessed July 12, 2024, https://sdgs.un.org

governance in preparing a foundation for business ethics and institutionalizing ethical decision-making in the organization.

Table 1.1	Evolution of business ethics (key milestones)

Year	Milestone
Pre-1987	Businesses historically integrated ethics into operations, focusing on employee care, biodiversity, and community impact.
1987	The Brundtland Commission Report introduces sustainable development, influencing business ethics.[4]
1990s-2000s	Governments enforce policies requiring businesses to address the social and environmental impacts of their operations.
2008	The Global Financial Crisis highlights the need for stronger business ethics due to widespread financial fraud.[5]
2015	The Sustainable Development Goals (SDGs) are established, emphasizing ethical practices in global business.[6]

1.2 Definition of Ethics

Ethics is derived from the Greek word "ethos," which means character. The Cambridge Dictionary defines ethics as "a system of accepted beliefs that control behavior."[7] Similarly, according to

---

4. "Brundtland Commission Report," World Commission for Sustainable Development, accessed July 12, 2024, https://sustainabledevelopment.un.org

5. M.K. Brunnermeier, "Deciphering the Liquidity and Credit Crunch 2007-2008," *Journal of Economic Perspectives* 23, no. 1 (2009): 77-100, https://doi.org/10.1257/jep.23.1.774o

6. "Sustainable Development Goals (SDGs) (Agenda 2030)," United Nations, accessed July 12, 2024, https://sdgs.un.org

7. "Ethics Definition," Cambridge Dictionary, accessed July 12, 2024, https://dictionary.cambridge.org

the Oxford Dictionary, ethics involve "the study of the concepts involved in practical reasoning."[8]

In simple words, ethics are behavioral expectations derived from people's beliefs. If one abides by these expectations, one is judged as ethical; if not, one is labeled unethical. For instance, corruption may be looked down upon by people in a society. Hence, any individual or business entity, involved in corruption would be unethical, according to the people in that society. Another example could be related to environmental protection. If society considers cutting down trees as absolutely wrong, irrespective of the needs and reasons behind the act, any business engaging in deforestation would be considered unethical.

The primary usage of ethics is defining what is right and what is wrong. But, naturally, there is judgment involved in adhering to ethics. Two inferences emerge from this explanation. The first inference is that no "absolute right or wrong" defines ethics in a universal context. Ethics are usually "contextually defined and explained."

Actions that may be right in a particular context may not be right in another. For instance, eating non-vegetarian food may be a norm in a specific society but unacceptable in a different culture. Another example could be that the legal age for drinking alcohol or getting married is different from one country to the other. Similarly, for a business organization, there cannot be a universal minimum wage applicable to businesses worldwide. The "context" plays an essential role in determining the minimum standards. We will dive deeper into the role of context in terms of tackling local ethical issues in Chapter Two, section 2.5.1.

The second inference is that judgments of right or wrong in ethics are determined and shaped by beliefs held by the "majority" of the people in society. Usually, there is a risk that minority voices may not be considered when determining right

---

8. "Ethics Definition," Oxford Dictionary, accessed July 12, 2024, https://www.oxfordreference.com

and wrong. For instance, what most people wear in a culture becomes a norm. People in that culture defying the norm may be considered problematic or threatening to that culture.

Table 1.2	Definitions of ethics
Definition Source	**Definition of Ethics**
Cambridge Dictionary[9]	A system of accepted beliefs that control behavior
Oxford Dictionary[10]	The study of the concepts involved in practical reasoning
General Concept	Behavioral expectations derived from people's beliefs

1.3 Need and Significance of Ethics

The need for and significance of ethics, specifically business ethics, can be discussed in various ways. Since ethics sustain societies, in the absence of ethics, there would be anarchy, conflict, and even war. Therefore, ethics bind people together through collective beliefs and contribute to peaceful coexistence.

The logic of ethics can be derived from religions across the world. People follow the ethics emerging from their respective faiths' teachings and doctrines. Business ethics are significant especially because businesses are one of the most influential stakeholders in a society. Given their sphere of influence, their impact is enormous on people's lives. This impact could be positive as well as harmful. To ensure that the effect is positive, business ethics become vital.

---

9. "Ethics Definition," Cambridge Dictionary, accessed July 12, 2024, https://dictionary.cambridge.org

10. "Ethics Definition," Oxford Dictionary, accessed July 12, 2024, https://www.oxfordreference.com

For example, the turnover of some of the top Fortune 500 companies is higher than the gross domestic product (GDP) of some countries.[11] Thus, unsustainable or unethical business operations of the former could harm a vast population in their country. Such operations may also generate ripple effects in other nations. Hence, given the scale of impact, business ethics are critical.

Apart from an altruistic motive, business ethics allow organizations to operate in society and carry out their economic activities smoothly. With global agendas like the Sustainable Development Goals and the Paris Agreement being pursued at international platforms, government plans, and policies have started incorporating social and environmental ethics in their desired objectives.

Businesses with effective, visionary leadership understand that they must conduct business ethically to sustain in the long term. Such business organizations focus on the needs of different stakeholders and prioritize ethical decision-making. These organizations stand the test of time and continue thriving in societies.

For instance, the recent COVID-19 pandemic tested the priorities and resilience of business organizations. While some organizations capitalized on the situation to make money, others went out of their way to support people at a critical point when their lives were at stake. Given the context of a pandemic, businesses that choose kindness and empathy over profit maximization are the ones viewed by society with respect and recognition, giving them a license to operate in the long term.

1.3.1 Why are ethics important in a company?

Business organizations are of many types. These include sole proprietorship concerns, partnership firms, and companies or corporations. In a sole proprietorship concern, the owner and

---

11. "McKinsey," effective 2021, https://www.mckinsey.com

manager are usually the same person. In this case, the owner's liability is unlimited, and the business has no separate legal entity. Therefore, ethical issues may be resolved by the whole and sole owner and manager of the organization.

In this case, business ethics are the same as the ethics of the business owner. The entire accountability is that of the owner, who may or may not make ethical decisions. In such a case, the law plays a significant role in enforcing the principles of "right" and "wrong." For instance, if a sole proprietor cheats on customers by selling contaminated products, there is hardly any check within the organization. However, the customers take legal action to seek justice and compensation.

In the case of a partnership firm, two or more partners come together to establish and run a business organization. These partners work and share profits on mutually agreed terms and conditions. The liability is unlimited in the case of partnership firms, and the personal values and morals of the partners also govern ethics. However, since more people are involved, having a framework or code of ethics for decision-making can be helpful. For example, if one partner is ethical and the other is unethical, the former can monitor the latter's activities. However, here the governance mechanisms are less sophisticated than a company form of organization.

Lastly, the "company" is a unique business organization with several stakeholders and competing interests. The management and ownership of a company may be held in different hands. Ethical frameworks and codified conduct can be vital for decision-making in such a case.

In a company, a group of people known as promoters contribute money, known as the capital. In a publicly listed company, which is a specific type of company listed on the stock exchange, the promoters issue an initial public offering to raise money from the public. Ethics in a publicly listed company are of utmost significance. This is especially because ownership and management are separated in such a company and many stakeholders are affected by the company's decisions.

The promoters and other representatives participate in the company's governance. A few promoters and managers hired as employees may manage the affairs, and any general public member can invest money. Other stakeholders include lenders, suppliers, employees, government, civil society organizations, community and media representatives. In the absence of standard operating procedures and clear frameworks for ethical decision-making, it shall be challenging to safeguard the interests of these varied stakeholders with competing interests.

For example, let us assume that a company engaged in information technology (IT) consulting has to decide whether to upskill its employees to use the latest artificial intelligence (AI) technologies to the company's advantage or to replace these people with such technologies. The ethical dilemma is whether the company should retrain employees or lay them off to be able to afford AI support.

The employee union in this company favors re-training, but the management is divided. Non-governmental organizations (NGOs) working in the labor dignity and rights domain support the employee union, while government policies are non-interfering since it is an internal matter of the company. Employee unrest is expected to cause a potential loss in shareholder value. Some members of the management feel that layoffs will not only hurt the company's brand image but will also create dissatisfaction among other employees and stakeholders.

As discussed in the above scenario, there are many stakeholders, and some of them expect contradictory decisions. Table 1.3 outlines the diverse expectations and potential conflicts among stakeholders in a company.

Table 1.3	Expectations and conflicts of stakeholders in a company

Stakeholder	Expectations	Possible Ethical Conflict or Concern
Shareholders	Return on investment, transparency	Short-term profit versus long-term sustainability
Employees	Fair wages, job security, working conditions	Layoffs, workplace safety, work-life balance
Suppliers	Timely payments, fair contracts	Pricing or contract terms
Community	Environmental and social impact	Resource usage, community displacement, empowerment
Government	Compliance with regulations, taxes	Regulatory compliance or evasion
Management	Profitability, strategic vision	Maximizing profits versus meeting stakeholders' expectations

As seen in the above table, the scope of expectations mismatch among various stakeholders in a company is quite high. Having an ethical decision-making framework based on the principle of maximization of benefits for the maximum number of stakeholders can institutionalize ethics in the organization and help in reaching a consensus. This principle is explained further in the subsequent section 1.5 of this chapter.

Such dilemmas and the need for decision-making to deal with these dilemmas are common in the company form of business organization. The following chapters discuss theories of ethics and frameworks for making ethical decisions that can help deal with such dilemmas.

1.4 Difference Between Ethics, Values, and Morals

The terms ethics, values, and morals may be used interchangeably but they denote different meanings. Ethics emerge from beliefs most people hold in a context, but values can be personal. On the other hand, morals are also judgments like ethics, but they operate at an individual level, like values.

Values indicate the preferences of an individual. A set of preferred values, arranged in order of intensity, forms a person's value system. These may include positive values such as honesty, courage, kindness, empathy, diversity, teamwork, commitment, discipline, integrity, and accountability. However, one may also prefer negative values like revenge, greed, manipulation, dishonesty, addiction, obsession, and so on.

Thus, values explain what an individual attaches "value" or "worth" to; these are personal and may not align with the ethics of the community. Values may not sync with the "rights" and "wrongs" as believed by society. They are preferences shaped by a person's upbringing, conditioning, reference groups or social circle, personal circumstances, and life experiences.

On the other hand, morals, like ethics, define "right" or "wrong" in a specific decision or situation. Morals are shaped by social influences, religion, and culture. However, ethics hold for most people in society, and morals function at an individual level, like values. This is why organizations develop the "code of ethics" and not the "code of morals." It implies that ethics are relatively more objective and universal than morals.

Table 1.4	Ethics, morals, and values

Concept	Definition
Ethics[12]	Norms and standards of behavior derived from collective beliefs, guiding what is considered right or wrong in society
Morals[13]	Individual judgments of right or wrong influenced by personal values, social factors, etc. in a certain situation
Values[14]	Personal preferences indicating what is valuable or worthy, shaped by family, individual experiences, culture, etc

In a business organization, while ethics govern right or wrong at the organizational level, morals operate at an individual level and the personal value systems of employees, suppliers, community representatives, lenders, managers, and other stakeholders may also play a role in decision-making.

According to one of the core principles of management, proposed by Henry Fayol, individuals in an organization must subordinate their interests to the organization's goals.[15] Thus, the business entity expects that ethics will supersede individual morals or values if these are conflicting in nature.

For example, let us say that a mining company begins operations in a new region. Due to these operations, the lives of community members in that region shall be affected in many ways. Besides the adverse effects of mining, there are positive outcomes as the mining company invests in Corporate Social Responsibility (CSR) activities. According to the code of conduct of this business, mining is an ethical activity. An employee who

---

12. L.K. Treviño and K.A. Nelson, *Managing Business Ethics: Straight Talk About How to Do It Right* (Wiley, 2017), 7th ed.

13. B. Gert, "Morality" in *The Stanford Encyclopedia of Philosophy* (Stanford University, 2005).

14. M. Rokeach, "The Nature of Human Values" (Free Press., 1973).

15. Henri Fayol, *14 Principles of Management*, accessed July 12, 2024, https://mmhapu.ac.in

believes mining is unsustainable may continue working in this organization driven by her financial needs. Her morals do not advocate for this work, but she abides by the organization's ethics and bears cognitive dissonance arising from this conflict.

To understand values, we may say that, in this particular scenario, the employee continues to work because she values "a good life" for her family, which depends on the monetary compensation given by the employer.

1.5 What Is an Ethical Company?

As we have discussed in section 1.1 previously, ethics are contextual. Ethics are defined according to the majority of people's beliefs in a specific context. Therefore, explaining an ethical company through a universal meaning is challenging.

To define an ethical company, we can consider positive and negative aspects. Defining the negative dimension is relatively more straightforward. It refers to task activities or behaviors the company must not undertake or exhibit, to be ethical.

For example, a company must not indulge in malpractices and illegal activities such as hoarding, corruption, or harassment or behave in ways that might be destructive to the community or the environment. Some of these activities may be illegal, while some may be legal but unethical. We will discuss the detailed difference between ethics and law in the next chapter.

Regarding the positive dimension, an ethical company can be defined using the lens of stakeholder theory. Edward Freeman, in 1988, proposed the stakeholder theory.[16] It is a widely used theory in business and management that explains business purpose and conduct. Deriving from this theory, an ethical company can be described as one focusing on fulfilling the needs of different

---

16. Edward R. Freeman, Daniel R. Gilbert, and Edward Hartman, "Values and the Foundations of Strategic Management," *Journal of Business Ethics*, no. 7 (1988): 821-834.

stakeholders and pursuing the goal of stakeholder wealth maximization. This means the company focuses on increasing the wealth of all stakeholders at large, by maximizing the market value of company shares.

Further learning (link also available in Online Resources)
"What is Stakeholder Theory?" https://bit.ly/41ovhm8

Traditionally, profit maximization has been mentioned as the prime goal of a business organization. However, empirical evidence shows that profit maximization is a narrow approach and does not lead to long-term profits and firms› sustainability. For example, a firm that prefers profit maximization over research and development activities will not be equipped to deal with rapidly changing technology, market trends, and volatile business environments.

Similarly, an organization may save by reducing salaries or training costs. Still, it will lose better employees in the long run, who will shift to organizations offering better training opportunities and compensation. Therefore, stakeholder wealth maximization is a better approach to running a business. Practically, it does not conflict with the profit maximization goal.

Thus, an ethical company does not indulge in malpractices, wrong-doings, or illegal activities of any kind. It integrates decision-making in its business model that recognizes "right" or "wrong" from the perspective of maximization of benefits, for a maximum number of stakeholders. A genuinely ethical company will also consider the environment, biodiversity conservation, and society, including the vulnerable and marginalized communities, in its list of stakeholders. Such companies spend considerable effort and time identifying their stakeholders, engaging with them regularly through appropriate strategies, and identifying issues of material significance to these stakeholders.

In the next chapter, we will explore business ethics fundamentals, including sources, perspectives, and theories.

Further learning (link also available in Online Resources)
"Ted Talk: Is Business Ethics an Oxymoron?" https://bit.ly/3CS8hT4

Discussion Questions

1. Ethics emerge from collective beliefs. How and why? Explain the difference between ethics and values.

2. Why do companies need to define ethics through a code? Is it necessary? Discuss.

3. What is the purpose of a company? How can ethics play a role in enabling a company to achieve its goals?

Chapter Summary

◆ Ethics define right and wrong based on collective beliefs held by the majority of people in a society.

◆ The concept of context is fundamental, as ethics may differ in different contexts.

◆ Ethics are based on most people's beliefs, while morals are based on personal values. Values may or may not carry the connotations of being right or wrong, but these are shaped by biology and social experiences.

◆ An ethical company does not engage in any negative behavior or malpractices. Further, such a company tries to achieve the goal of stakeholder wealth maximization in line with the stakeholder theory.

◆ Companies must pay significant attention to ethics because ownership and management are separated in such organizations. Shareholders have limited liability, but the board of directors' decisions impact a wide range of stakeholders.

Quiz

1. **What does the term business refer to in the context of business ethics?**

    a. Providing employment opportunities

    b. Buying and selling goods and services for profit

    c. Fulfilling unmet needs

    d. Undertaking corporate social responsibility activities

2. **In a sole proprietorship, who typically resolves ethical issues?**

    a. The board of directors

    b. The stakeholders

    c. The sole owner and manager

    d. The employees

3. **What do ethics refer to in the context of business ethics?**

    a. Legal requirements that must be followed

    b. Norms and standards based on society's beliefs

    c. Profit-making strategies

    d. Government regulations

4. **Business ethics started gaining significance after which major event?**

    a. The Industrial Revolution

    b. The 2008 subprime crisis

    c. The Brundtland Commission Report

    d. The introduction of Sustainable Development Goals

5. **What does the term 'ethos' mean in Greek?**

    a. Beliefs

    b. Society

    c. Character

    d. Culture

6. **Which report defined sustainable development as meeting the needs of the present without compromising the ability of future generations?**

    a. Brundtland Commission Report

    b. The Kyoto Protocol

    c. The Paris Agreement

    d. The World Economic Forum Report

7. **According to the Cambridge Dictionary, what is ethics?**

    a. A system of accepted beliefs that control behavior

    b. The study of the concepts involved in practical reasoning

    c. Norms and standards derived from legal requirements

    d. A set of laws governing right and wrong

8. **Which of the following is an example of an unethical business activity?**

    a. Engaging in corruption

    b. Investing in research and development

    c. Conducting CSR activities

    d. Expanding through diversification

9. **What is the primary usage of ethics in society?**

   a. Defining profit-making strategies

   b. Regulating market development

   c. Defining what is right and wrong

   d. Governing government regulations

10. **Which of the following statements is true about ethics?**

    a. Ethics are universally defined and absolute.

    b. Ethics are contextually defined and explained.

    c. Ethics are based on individual preferences.

    d. Ethics do not overlap with legal requirements.

Answers	1 – b	2 – c	3 – b	4 – c	5 – c
	6 – a	7 – a	8 – a	9 – c	10 – b

This page is intentionally left blank

Chapter **2**

Theoretical Foundations of Business Ethics

> ### KEY LEARNING OBJECTIVES
>
> - Explain different sources of ethical decisions.
> - Share some insight on the evolution of ethics.
> - Distinguish between ethics and law.
> - Describe different theoretical perspectives related to ethics.

This chapter provides critical insight into different perspectives and theories of ethics. Ethics may be derived from culture, science, religion, biology, and law. However, ethics and law may not always overlap. Some decisions are ethical but illegal, while some are legal but unethical. We will discuss such differences and contradictions in this chapter, with the help of practical examples.

Apart from these perspectives, we explain the key ethical philosophies from which the theories of ethics emerge. We see how ethics are derived from two philosophies - deontology and teleology, leading to different theoretical perspectives such as duty ethics, utilitarianism, virtue ethics, and care ethics. Further, we cover these theories in detail to understand why different people believe in different ethical choices. The theories highlight contrasts as well as consensus in beliefs.

As discussed in the last chapter, ethics determine right or wrong based on the collective opinions, and beliefs within the context in which the business operates. Ethics are not about the personal or individual beliefs of managers, employees, or the board of directors. There is a degree of universality, but ethics are not absolute; they may change with a change in context. Understanding different sources, perspectives, and ethics theories can help make decisions in various business situations.

2.1 Sources of Ethics

Ethics are derived from different sources, as discussed in this section. It is fascinating to observe that even biologically, human beings are designed to be ethical. Researchers in neurosciences, psychology, and sociology have provided evidence on how our bodies are designed to behave ethically and choose the right option over the wrong.[17] Therefore, human bodies and minds are the primary sources of ethics in society.

For instance, mirror neurons in our brains enable us to experience empathy. This is why one may cry watching an emotional movie despite knowing it is fiction, a story. Empathy makes us human and helps us make the right decisions. Scientists also believe that those with highly empathetic personalities have a bigger amygdala, a tiny, almond-shaped structure in the brain.[18]

---

17. "Neuroethics: Enabling and Enhancing Neuroscience Advances for Society," NIH BRAIN Initiative, accessed July 15, 2024, https://braininitiative.nih.gov/

18. B. Brierley, P. Shaw P, and A.S. David, "The human amygdala: a systematic review and meta-analysis of volumetric magnetic resonance imaging," *Brain Res Brain Res Rev.* 39, no. 1 (2002): 84-105, doi: 10.1016/s0165-0173(02)00160-1

Similarly, reflexes and senses are also designed for humans to experience emotions such as disgust or guilt. These emotions can motivate one to choose an ethical option, even if it is the most difficult. However, everyone may not follow these instincts or experience these emotions. Deviations may be linked to changes in biological, social, and environmental situations, life experiences, or the availability of rewards.

Another source of ethics is religion. Different religions worldwide provide insight for distinguishing between right and wrong decisions. Some religious doctrines are universal, while some may be specific to a particular religion. Religion shapes beliefs, and shared beliefs comprise culture.

In some instances, ethics can also be linked to culture. For example, ethics related to personal space or privacy, hair or clothing, marriages or relationships with family members, festivals, or rituals may emerge from the culture of a specific community. Whatever may be right in one context may not be so in the other.

For instance, white-colored wedding clothes are worn by brides in Western contexts, while red is the preferred color in the Indian context. In some communities, families prefer staying in large families, while nuclear families may be the norm in others. The ethics emerging from culture may result from a social contract between people. It implies that people tend to abide by community ethics so that each one continues to receive support from the other.

Figure 2.1	Sources of ethics

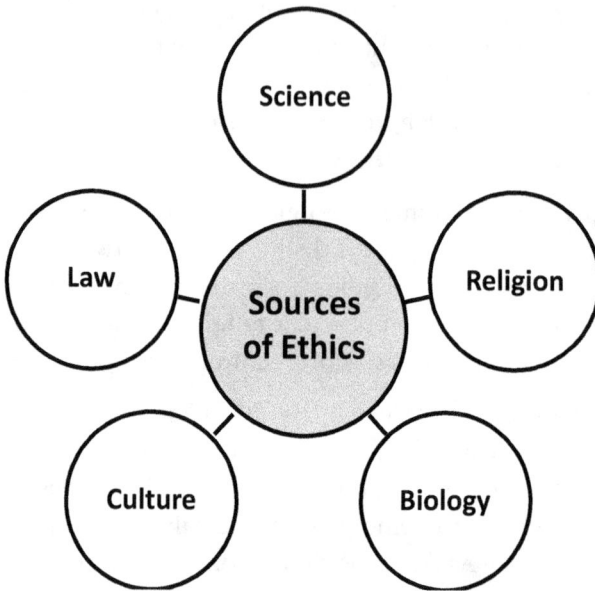

Finally, law can also be a source of ethics. This happens when legal obligations and ethical recommendations overlap. For instance, cheating customers is wrong both legally and ethically. However, laws related to competition may be different across countries. Section 2.5 provides more details on ethics and laws.

Business ethics are derived from all these sources and codified to enable stakeholders to understand decision-making in the respective organization. The better the clarity in the code of ethics, the fewer the conflicts related to ethics, because the code helps in evidence-based decision-making.

In the subsequent section, we discuss different perspectives and theories to understand the theoretical foundations of ethics. An insight into such perspectives and theories provides fundamental knowledge on understanding ethical dilemmas and making decisions in difficult situations.

2.2 Different Perspectives of Ethics

Historically, there have been different phases related to ethics. These phases were marked by war, political turmoil, economic crisis, or a massive corporate scandal.

Aristotle's Nicomachean Ethics, written almost 2000 years ago, explains ethics as virtues required for a good living.[19] Such virtues are not theoretical ideas for contemplation but practical, day-to-day habits. In Asia, Kautilya wrote the *Arthashastra* in the fourth century B.C.[20] He talked about value-based leadership derived from the ideals of truthfulness, righteousness, gratefulness, and reliability. There was also Karl Marx, who questioned capitalism. In his words, capitalism "sows the seeds of its own destruction" by delineating the masses and exploiting the working class.[21]

While such references have been critical to developing the present-day narrative on business ethics, teaching ethics in business schools is relatively new. It started in the 1970s in American business schools, where many business education ideas and practices originated and spread globally. Most literature on business ethics is the product of the late twentieth century.[22]

Renowned author Peter Drucker, the Father of Modern Management, wrote a paper in 1980 titled - "What is Business Ethics?"[23] He referred to the rapid pace at which business ethics became an "in subject," and business schools and universities introduced it as a standalone course. He strongly criticized business ethics as "no ethics at all" and considered the value no more than "society gossip." The criticism, which has continued till date, began when business schools introduced ethics courses.

---

19. "Nicomachean Ethics," Aristotle, accessed July 12, 2024, https://www.academia.edu

20. N.S. Kumar and U.S. Rao, "Guidelines for Value Based Management in Kautilya's Arthashastra," *Journal of Business Ethics*, no. 15 (1996): 415-423, https://link.springer.com

21. "Marxism," David L. Prychitko, accessed July 12, 2024, https://www.econlib.org

22. "Cambridge University Press," Gabriel Abend, accessed July 20, 2024, https://www.cambridge.org

23. Peter F. Drucker, "What is Business Ethics?," *The Public Interest* 63, no. 2 (1981): 18-36.

In between, when corporate scandals like Enron happened, those voicing for business ethics came to the forefront. A similar situation occurred during events like the financial crisis of 2008.[24]

In 2022, the debate heated up again in the post-pandemic world. The question is – "Why do business ethics matter now?" Nobel Laureate economist Amartya Sen wrote a paper on this topic in 1993, vividly describing how denying business ethics is impractical.[25] In his words, business ethics can be "crucially important in economic organizations." Humans are naturally ethical; biologists advocate this idea by discussing mirror neurons.[26] So, if individuals or organizations are unethical, it is by conscious choice and not by default because otherwise, there will be chaos. Ethics create benefits, including customer faith, market reputation, supplier support, and trust from stakeholders like the government, civil society, and the media. Ultimately, to the firm, all of this makes solid business sense. No matter the challenges, such organizations survive and thrive in the long run.

2.3 Philosophies of Ethics

To begin with, we shall discuss two primary philosophies from which ethics emerge in society. These philosophies are deontology and teleology.[27] Deontology has been derived from the Greek word *"deont,"* meaning binding, and teleology from the Greek word *"telos,"* meaning end.[28]

Deontological ethics imply that the moral value of the decision is more important than the consequences achieved from that

---

24. Paul H. Dembinski, Carole Lager, Andrew Cornford, and Jean-Michel Bonvin, *Enron and World Finance: A Case Study in Ethics* (Palgrave Macmillan UK, 2006), https://link.springer.com

25. Amartya Sen, "Does Business Ethics Make Economic Sense?," *Business Ethics Quarterly* 3, no. 1 (1993): 45-54, https://www.jstor.org

26. "Mirror Neurons," accessed July 12, 2024, https://www.ncbi.nlm.nih.gov

27. Warren Ashby, "Teleology and Deontology in Ethics," *The Journal of Philosophy* 47, no. 26 (1950): 765–73, https://doi.org/10.2307/2020659

28. "Deontology Definition," accessed July 12, 2024, https://www.etymonline.com

decision. On the other hand, teleological ethics means that the decision choice depends on the value of the consequences associated with each decision.[29] Ethics are absolute in the former philosophy, while ethics are subjective in the latter.

This means that in deontology, ethical choices are the only way to live. Still, in teleology, one can evaluate the choices, weigh the outcomes, and make a decision that suits most stakeholders because the ends justify the means. For example, deontology can be explained in terms of following one religion. The believer of that religion must follow all the rituals or apply all the learnings prescribed by that religion without questioning the outcomes. However, in teleology, one may choose to be secular and make choices to benefit the maximum number of people.

In the case of business ethics, let's say a construction company has to evaluate a proposal to set up a hospital by demolishing a religious place. Suppose the company follows a deontological perspective, and its code of ethics considers demolishing religious buildings or structures unethical. In that case, the company will not consider this proposal, irrespective of the costs and benefits associated with this proposition.

However, suppose that the company follows a teleological perspective. In that case, the costs and benefits associated with all the options will be evaluated by the management. The final decision will be the one agreed to by a maximum number of stakeholders so that gains for all the parties are maximized.

2.4 Theories of Ethics

Two major theories of ethics emerge from these philosophies: duty ethics and utilitarianism. These theories are discussed in the following section:

---

29. "Teleological Ethics," accessed July 12, 2024, https://www.britannica.com

2.4.1 Duty ethics

Duty Ethics, emerging from deontology, comprises the body of knowledge proposed and led by philosophers like Immanuel Kant.[30] According to this theory, ethical choices are duties. One must fulfill these obligations irrespective of the consequences while living in a society. For example, one must vote in a democracy regardless of one's liking or disliking of contemporary politics or eat vegetarian food if prescribed by one's religion.

From a business perspective, one must contribute to community development initiatives through CSR programs because the business considers it to be its duty to give back to the community. Not because it shall create a positive brand image or because it is a legal obligation.

> Further learning (link also available in Online Resources)
> **"Immanuel Kant"** https://bit.ly/4gC5zyR

2.4.2 Utilitarianism

Utilitarianism, on the other hand, emerges from teleology.[31] In utilitarianism, the action that creates the greatest good or utility for the most significant number of people is the right, ethical option. "Good" here refers to utility, value, benefit, happiness, or any similar form of positive outcomes. According to this theory, decision-making involves listing all options and evaluating the benefits of each option. The option that creates the maximum net positive benefit for maximum stakeholders is to be selected.

Let us consider the example of a business organization that has the option to decide whether or not it should shift to a more environmentally friendly technology. One option is to continue with the existing technology. This is currently beneficial in terms of cost but can lead to higher costs in the long run. Expected changes in competitors' moves and government policies indicate

---

30. "Duty Ethics," accessed July 12, 2024, https://www.philosophos.org
31. "Utilitarianism Theory," accessed July 12, 2024, https://plato.stanford.edu

that the company will eventually have to shift to the new technology.

If the company does so under pressure later, it will lose out on reputation, economies of scale, and first-mover advantage. Considering a holistic appraisal of the situation, the company will benefit from shifting to the new technology in the long run. It will reduce costs and generate brand equity and government support. Thus, using the utility concept, investing in new technology will be the better option.

This implies that benefits in this theory are only sometimes evaluated in terms of financial gains in the short term. One must consider the net positive benefit created for the firm in the long run. However, assessing outcomes takes work, and some degree of subjectivity may be involved. Further, while considering the stakeholders, this approach may not favor the minority, vulnerable, and marginalized stakeholders.

Apart from these theories, two more theoretical approaches are discussed in the literature. They are known as virtue ethics and ethics of care.

> Further learning (link also available in Online Resources)
> **"What is Utilitarianism"** https://bit.ly/3X0b5Vh

2.4.3 Virtue ethics

Virtue ethics explain that one must choose virtue over anything.[32] This means that neither duties nor outcomes affect ethical choices; what matters is the intention and effort to lead a virtuous life. One selects an option because this is the person one wants to be, regardless of whether it is one's duty or leads to beneficial outcomes.

For example, a teacher who tries to be empathetic to the students has chosen to be so because she feels this is how she

---

32. "Virtue Ethics," accessed July 12, 2024, https://plato.stanford.edu

wants to be. It has nothing to do with the expectations of society or the benefits of her empathy for students. In a business context, a firm may operate in a geographical location where business owners present gifts to politicians. They may not be paying them money, but offering gifts in kind. In such cases, the business owner may not agree to this culture because they want to be an entrepreneur who builds their venture without engaging in any form of corruption. They do not agree to present gifts because they believe it is equally unethical.

2.4.4 Care ethics

Care ethics are ethics based on compassion, empathy, care, and similar values.[33] They are different from other theories of ethics. Usually, one relies on reason, rationale, or logic while explaining ethical choices. In duty ethics, the purpose is fulfilling obligations. In utilitarianism, value maximization is the goal. Character building and leading a virtuous life are the primary outcomes of virtue ethics. However, one can make exceptional decisions in care ethics because the situation demands human values, emotions, nurturing, and a caring attitude.

For example, one may choose to provide benefits to a minority group because they come from an economically disadvantaged section of society and need support, to be at par with financially advantaged groups. In a business scenario, one may make exceptions in lending procedures if one feels the client needs support in a difficult time. However, if the organization relies on care ethics to make decisions, favoritism, nepotism, and undue advantage are the associated risks.

---

33. "Ethics of Care," accessed July 12, 2024, https://plato.stanford.edu

Figure 2.2	Theories of ethics

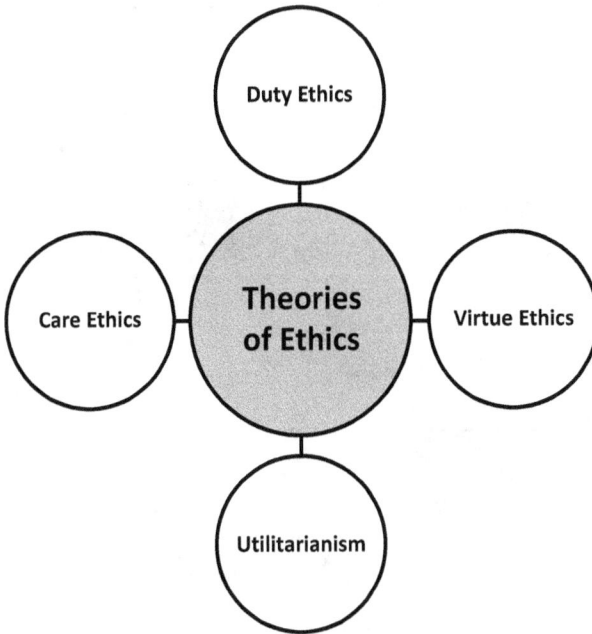

2.5 Ethics and Law

Ethics and laws can be represented through a Venn diagram wherein some decisions are ethical and legal, some are ethical but illegal, and some are legal but unethical. Where laws become silent or provide limited guidance, ethics must be referred to when making decisions. Unlike the laws, ethics are not enforced by the court of law. Laws and ethics are similar in one way; as laws are also restricted to a geographic location by jurisdiction, while local beliefs shape ethics.

Figure 2.3　Ethics and Law

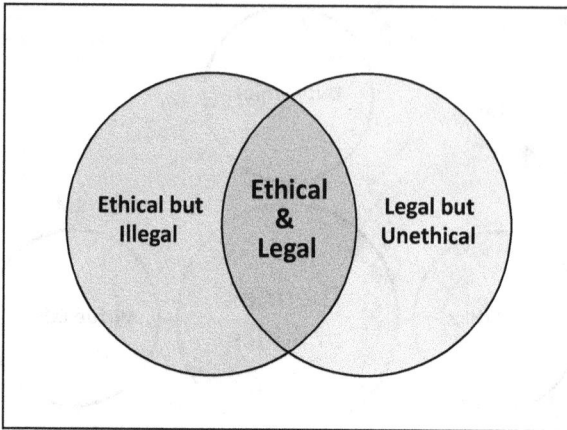

Let us consider the hiring decisions in a business organization. Hiring is an organization's internal matter, especially in the private sector. The human resource department may recruit and select candidates aligning with the company's policies. However, there could be a law in the region where the business is located that mandates the company to reserve a percentage of vacancies for minorities - people of specific origin or gender. Fulfilling requirements under this law would be a legal decision. It will also be ethical if the community believes reservation helps promote minority interests in that region.

Let us assume that another law allows the company to pay different wages to employees based on their religion. Hiring and compensating according to this law is a legal decision but may not be ethical as the community may consider this as discrimination against a specific religion. Similarly, if the employees stage a protest against this law, it may be regarded as illegal. However, it would be an ethical move in the eyes of the employees benefiting from this law.

The conflict between ethics and laws can give rise to ethical dilemmas. One such dilemma could be the case of a worker who was drunk while operating a heavy machine. The worker had been intoxicated on some occasions in the past too, but managed to complete his job satisfactorily. However, this time, he committed a mistake that led to him losing his life. He left behind his wife and three children, who hoped to receive compensation from the company since he died at his workplace.

In this case, knowing that the worker was drunk, the management may deny compensation. However, the supervisor knows the family has no other earning source, and the compensation can help the daily members rebuild their lives. The worker who lost his life was also a close friend. In this situation, laws and ethics contradict each other, giving rise to a specific dilemma. The decision to compensate may be ethical but not legal, while denying compensation is legal but it may not be ethical.

In this section, we saw some scenarios where ethics and laws conflicted based on local circumstances. Let's look at how businesses can tackle such scenarios in the next section.

2.5.1 Going "Glocal"—Global exposure and local alignment

As discussed in Chapter One, section 1.2, context is key in evaluating the ethical validity of a manager's decision-making outcomes. Local context determines what is considered ethical and what is not. As the world increasingly operates through global delivery models, and internet connectivity makes cross-border business commonplace, managers may face conflicts while navigating ethical dilemmas in different cultural contexts. At times, they may make decisions that simultaneously affect multiple cultures—where the same choice is well-received in one culture but not in the other.

To summarize, decision-making in cross-border organizations may be complex due to multiple factors:

- Some decisions are influenced by legal requirements that differ across countries, such as minimum wage laws.
- Cultural differences, like workplace attire norms, shape some decisions

- Some situations create ethical dilemmas, where local practices conflict with organizational values (e.g., differential pay based on nationality) or personal values (e.g., displacement of local communities due to business activities).

Let's take the example of a Fast-Moving Consumer Goods (FMCG) company operating across multiple countries. Food labeling regulations vary from nation to nation—the permitted sugar content, the class of preservatives allowed, and the flexibility to choose core ingredients differ based on local laws. In such a case, how does a manager decide what is ethical and what is not?

By law, every company must comply with the legal requirements of the country in which it operates. However, the decision to go beyond legal compliance and uphold ethical standards in all contexts is guided by the company's code of conduct, decision-making framework, and core organizational values.

An ethical company considers the world as one and avoids practices like greenwashing—where the ethical burden of one geographical context, often the more developed one, is shifted onto another, usually the less developed. As a manager, one may face situations where local business practices do not align with personal values. In such cases, as an organizational representative, the expectation is to prioritize organizational ethics over personal beliefs.

While legal compliance is non-negotiable, cultural adaptations require a balanced approach. In such cases, managers should refer to the organization's ethical philosophy—whether it follows a teleological or deontological framework. Managers can apply ethical decision-making tests to evaluate their options if a situation not explicitly covered in the company's code of conduct arises. We will explore tests for ethical decision-making in detail as part of Chapter Three.

Thus, global ethics are not about imposing uniformity but aligning ethical integrity with local realities, i.e. "going *glocal.*" This requires global awareness and experience, and a local alignment and application.

In the next chapter, we will discuss the frameworks for making ethical decisions emerging from the perspectives and theories covered in this chapter.

Discussion Questions

1. Distinguish between ethics and law. State examples of decisions that are ethical but illegal and vice versa.

2. Discuss Peter Drucker's viewpoint on the discipline of business ethics.

3. Elaborate on the core principles of utilitarianism and duty ethics.

4. When do care ethics make sense? Explain with an example.

Chapter Summary

◆ Ethics can be derived from various sources, including biology, law, culture, religion, and science.

◆ Ethics have been explained by philosophers throughout history, including Aristotle, Karl Marx, Peter Drucker, and Kautilya.

◆ Ethics may overlap with law. However, some decisions are ethical but illegal, and vice versa.

◆ Ethics emerge from two philosophies, i.e. deontology, and teleology.

◆ There are four major theories of ethics - duty ethics, utilitarianism, virtue ethics, and care ethics.

◆ Duty ethics make ethical choices an obligation. As per utilitarianism, ethical choices bring maximum benefit to maximum people. Virtue ethics help in character building, and care ethics emerge from care, compassion, and empathy for others.

Quiz

1. **Which of the following ethical sources are mirror neurons related to?**

    a. Religion

    b. Culture

    c. Biology

    d. Law

2. **Which of the following is a biological structure associated with empathy?**

    a. Amygdala

    b. Hippocampus

    c. Thalamus

    d. Cerebellum

3. **Ethics derived from cultural norms are often a result of:**

    a. Legal mandates

    b. Social contracts

    c. Religious teachings

    d. Personal preferences

4. **An example of ethics derived from religion would be:**

    a. Environmental laws

    b. Tax regulations

    c. Dietary restrictions

    d. Cultural dress codes

5. **Which of the following is true about the relationship between ethics and law?**

    a. All legal actions are ethical.

    b. Ethics are enforced by the court of law.

    c. Ethics and laws never overlap.

    d. Some decisions can be ethical but illegal.

6. **A situation where paying different wages based on religion is considered:**

    a. Ethical and legal

    b. Ethical but illegal

    c. Legal but unethical

    d. Illegal and unethical

7. **When laws provide limited guidance, decision-makers should refer to:**

    a. Corporate policies

    b. Ethics

    c. Financial gains

    d. Stakeholder opinions

8. **Who proposed "Nicomachean Ethics," one of the early works on ethics?**

    a. Immanuel Kant

    b. Karl Marx

    c. Aristotle

    d. Peter Drucker

9. **Which philosopher's work is known for questioning capitalism and its ethical implications?**

   a. Kautilya

   b. Immanuel Kant

   c. Peter Drucker

   d. Karl Marx

10. **Who is the Father of Modern Management and critiqued business ethics in his 1980 paper?**

    a. Peter Drucker

    b. Amartya Sen

    c. Aristotle

    d. Kautilya

Answers	1 – c	2 – a	3 – b	4 – c	5 – d
	6 – c	7 – b	8 – c	9 – d	10 – a

Chapter **3**

Ethical Decision-Making

KEY LEARNING OBJECTIVES

- Assimilate the complexity and significance of decision-making in business organizations.
- Identify ethical dilemmas in business situations.
- Understand organizational frameworks for ethical decision-making.
- Apply different tests for ethical decision-making.

In this chapter, we cover the basics of ethical decision-making, since ethics are subjective and challenging to implement. The chapter provides insight for those interested in business management. This guidance helps resolve ethical dilemmas that managers face on a day-to-day basis.

In the absence of an ethical decision-making framework in a business organization, personal biases and errors may affect outcomes. Thus, we explain how organizations must extend efforts toward institutionalizing ethical frameworks. To guide managers in making ethical decisions, we discuss various tests and tools that can be used individually or in combination. When balanced together effectively, they ultimately lead to stakeholders' wealth maximization.

3.1 Introduction to Decision-Making in Business Organizations

We have discussed different philosophies and theories of ethics in the last chapter. In this chapter, we shall see how to apply ethical decision-making in a business context.

According to Koontz and O'Donnell, in their famous book titled "Principles of Management," managers perform five different functions.[34] These functions include planning, organizing, staffing, directing, and controlling. While performing these functions, managers have to make decisions day in and day out. Thus, the effectiveness of a manager is determined by their ability to make timely decisions related to these functions. This involves creating a positive impact with the least amount of resources.

From another perspective shared by Henry Mintzberg, managers perform three different roles in their jobs. They are interpersonal, informational, and decisional roles. In the decisional role, managers undertake a variety of tasks as entrepreneurs. These tasks are disturbance handling, resource allocation, and negotiation.[35]

Thus, decision-making is the essence of management. One usually competes to save time and money in the real world to achieve multi-stakeholder objectives like reputation management, community engagement, supplier support, employee welfare, and government support, almost simultaneously. Thus, a manager must not just make the right decisions but must make these

---

34. "Principles of Management," Harold Koontz and Cyril O'Donnell, effective 1968, https://ebrary.net
35. Henry Mintzberg, *The Nature of Managerial Work* (1973).

decisions in the least amount of time with the least possible resources.

To support managers in effective decision-making, organizations may have Standard Operating Procedures (SOPs). With the increasing use and application of Artificial Intelligence (AI), these procedures are gaining further ground. However, decision-making criteria and methodologies are different across organizations, even within the same industry. These depend on the organizational origin, history, evolution, leadership, type of business, geographical location, company scale, government regulations, and several other factors.

Even in organizations with well-defined policies, procedures, and by-laws, the subjectivity of managers plays a key role in decision-making. Thus, choosing the right option in these complex situations makes a manager's job challenging.

In this chapter, we shall discuss ethical dilemmas that may arise while evaluating decisions in business organizations, frameworks that may be useful in making ethical choices, and tests that can be applied to identify such decisions.

3.2 Ethical Dilemmas in Business Organizations

A business organization, particularly a joint stock company, affects and is affected by multiple stakeholders. Business stakeholders often fight a zero-sum game where the loss for one stakeholder would mean a gain for the other. Resource constraints and subjectivity exacerbate the challenges. In such scenarios, managers as decision-makers, face dilemmas while choosing the right option. These situations are known as ethical dilemmas.[36]

To understand ethical dilemmas in businesses better, let us take an example of construction workers working on-site, in extreme

---

36. O.C. Ferrell, John Fraedrich, and Linda Ferrell, *Business Ethics: Ethical Decision Making and Cases* (Dreamtech Press, 2005).

weather conditions for a company. For instance, let's assume the weather department issued a red alert that an intense heat wave would engulf the city over the next few days. Since the workers are engaged outdoors, they will bear the brunt of this harsh weather.

In the quarterly stakeholder meeting on the day of the forecast, one of the not-for-profit sector representatives raised this concern. The representative proposed shutting down the business operations for a week to safeguard the workers. This solution has varied implications for different stakeholders. The company may lose on time and miss the deadline. There might also be problems related to inventory management, maintenance, and continuity. The suppliers shall have to support the supply-chain disruptions.

In this case, the government may take a neutral, pro-worker, or pro-industry stance, depending on its ideology. The same goes for the employees. The media and civil society representatives shall appreciate the concern displayed by the company. One may assume that workers may appreciate this move. However, in some contexts, the workers may be operating on daily wages for the construction work. In such a case, the workers for whose benefit the work is being interrupted or stalled may not welcome this initiative. The managers in this scenario face an ethical dilemma, and their role is to make the right choice. One may shut down work, continue, or find a balance between the two options.

Managers face ethical dilemmas quite often in their jobs. These could be categorized in different ways. One way would be to look at ethical dilemmas from the perspective of different stakeholders, i.e. labor issues, community problems, employee concerns, supplier problems, shareholder grievances, and so on. This has been explained in the Table 3.1 below:

| Table 3.1 | Types of ethical dilemmas from stakeholders' perspective |

Category	Example	Stakeholders Involved
Labour Issues	Extreme weather conditions affecting construction workers	Workers, employers, government, community, suppliers
Community Problems	Pollution caused by factory operations	Local residents, environmental groups, government
Employee Concerns	Discrimination in hiring practices	Employees, human resource department, legal entities
Supplier Problems	Late payments affecting supplier operations	Suppliers, company, customers
Shareholder Grievances	Decisions impacting short-term vs long-term profitability	Shareholders, management, employees

(Source: Shaw, 1998)[37]

Further learning (link also available in Online Resources)
"Ethical Dilemma: Whose Life is More Valuable?"
https://bit.ly/3X3VAfO

The second way to classify dilemmas could be by identifying the function of management from which the dilemma emerges, such as finance, marketing, sales, human resource management, operations, etc. For instance, supply chain ethics issues may be related to testing products on animals in the cosmetic industry or using refined sugar or palm oil to manufacture products in the fast-moving consumer goods industry.

HRM concerns could be about hiring an inclusive workforce, designing compensation, or a leave policy that acknowledges the diversity among the workforce. Financial ethics issues could be concerning raising money from investors who may not value the long-term valuation of the firm or about selecting an internal or

---

37. William H. Shaw, *Moral Issues in Business* (1998).

external auditor. Marketing concerns may include selecting ethical brand names, designing clean labels, ensuring transparency in advertising, and so on.

The third way to categorize dilemmas could be from a legal standpoint. Some dilemmas may be legal but unethical or vice-versa. For instance, if two employees score the same in a selection process, how does the manager pick the right candidate? Let us assume that the manager belongs to the same city as one of the candidates. In this case, picking one of them shall be a difficult decision for the manager. However, the solution to most ethical decisions lies at the intersection of the decision areas, the disciplines, and the objectives involved.

To begin with, the company's legal documents may guide the selection of the right option. Then, the laws of the land could be referred to understand the ethical choice. Suppose either of these does not provide an answer, then the managers will have an easier way out in a company that has established an ethical framework for decision-making and communicated it to the employees.

This framework may be available in the policy documents shared with employees on joining or during training programs. The application of this framework shall be reflected in the decisions made by the organization in the past. By institutionalizing a framework in this way, decision-making may be clear, along with the prerogative of the manager responsible for the decision.

Having learned how to identify ethical dilemmas in business, as seen in this section, one can proceed to the next steps in ethical decision-making, as shown in Figure 3.1 below:

| Figure 3.1 | **Ethical decision-making** |

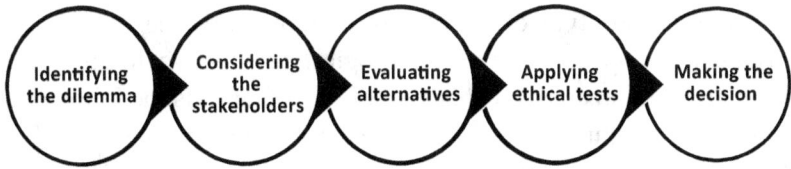

Identifying the dilemma → Considering the stakeholders → Evaluating alternatives → Applying ethical tests → Making the decision

In the upcoming sections, we will delve into the frameworks and ethical tests for effective decision-making in organizations.

3.3 Organizational Frameworks for Ethical Decision-Making

As discussed in section 2.4 of Chapter Two, the two primary philosophies of ethics, teleology, and deontology, give rise to two types of organizational frameworks: "utilitarianism" and "rules-based" ethics.[38] The first framework, "utilitarianism" is derived from the principles of teleology or outcomes. This framework is based on the concept that in an organizational context, the right choice brings maximum benefit to the maximum number of people.

Let us take the same example of construction laborers who work outdoors in peak summers and face the acute risk of heatstroke. In an organization where utilitarianism is institutionalized, the managers will try to select an option to maximize output for the maximum number of workers. Thus, the manager shall neither close operations, nor let them work without any intervention. For instance, one balanced solution could be to provide restrooms, oral rehydration solutions, and safety equipment, as well as restrict shift timings to early morning or late evening hours for a few days. In this way, one can create

---

38. Barbara MacKinnon, *Ethics: Theory and Contemporary Issues* (1995).

options that do not necessarily lead to loss for one and gain for the other.

In the second type of "rules-based" framework, the organization may rely on a deontological perspective. In this type, the organization creates a set of rules that must be followed to select the right choices. Irrespective of the outcomes and the costs or benefits associated with these outcomes, the right choice shall be guided by the decision-making rules framed by the organization. In the same example, the manager may shut down the business operations for a week if the organizational rules indicate a strong pro-worker ethic. On the other hand, the manager may continue with the status quo if the organizational rules do not support this action.

Figure 3.2   **Ethical decision-making frameworks**

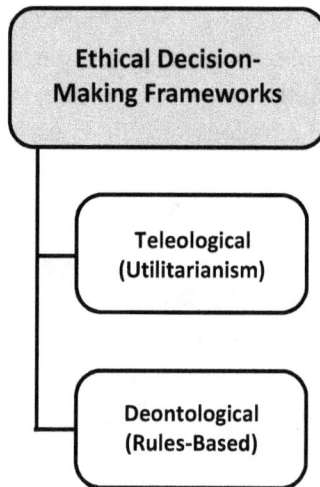

Ethical Decision-Making Frameworks

Teleological (Utilitarianism)

Deontological (Rules-Based)

The principles of ethical frameworks in business organizations shall be reflected in the vision and mission of the organization. Then, the company objectives shall also consider the repercussions of ethical choices. Finally, the policies, procedures, and rules shall all incorporate the framework's elements. The framework in detail may be found in the code of ethics, code of conduct, or a similar document.

In some organizations, a separate department may be established for ethical compliance, quality control, or business excellence. This helps institutionalize the ethical decision-making framework through documentation, training, and culture. The role of top management is crucial in this regard. The actions of leaders and their ethical choices deeply impact the choices made by employees. Chapter Six of this book sheds light on the role of leadership and corporate governance in promoting business ethics.

In addition to the frameworks discussed in this section, one can refer to different types of tests for ethical decision-making at an individual level. These tests are explained in the next section.

3.4 Tests for Ethical Decision-Making

Since ethical dilemmas are challenging and confusing, one can apply the following tests to select the right choice when confronted with right and wrong options.[39]

3.4.1 Viral news test

The viral news test enables one to make the right choice by assuming, whether or not one will be comfortable with the decision if the news of the decision goes viral. Let us assume that the decision is now known to everyone; would it make the person uncomfortable? Would one try to hide one's choice? If the answer is yes, it indicates that it is not the right choice, and one must avoid it. The viral news test is also known as the "grandmother or spouse test." If one is comfortable sharing the decision with one's grandmother or partner, one may go ahead.

---

39. "Tests for Ethical Decision-Making," accessed July, 2024, https://www.ethicsops.com

Viral news test conforms to the majority's viewpoint. It is helpful to make a decision that is in sync with the values of the society in which one lives. However, it may not take into account the viewpoint of minorities. Viral news tests promote compliance with societal ethics, even if one believes that sometimes one may take a different stance, to protect the interests of minority groups or lead a change in society.

Suppose "A" is a marketing executive in XYZ Limited. A's job profile involves traveling to meet clients. A is reimbursed for the travel expenses and must submit bills supporting the claim. "B," a colleague of A, advises A to inflate the bills by bribing the travel agent or using fake bills to get higher claim amounts. B insists that A does this, citing that it is a common practice among employees.

In this scenario, out of peer pressure, A might feel obligated to abide by what B suggests. However, by applying the viral news test in this situation, A can not only find one's answer but also try to convince B about the consequences of the virality of this news. If A does not want to be known as someone who submits fake bills to the company, A must not do it. Thus, the viral news test suggested submitting the actual bills for the claim.

The viral news test can also be applied to classic cases of financial fraud where business leaders try their best to conceal window dressing until it gets known to the media, the general public, and all stakeholders. If they were right, they wouldn't hide it.

3.4.2 Outcomes test

The second test is derived from the principles of utilitarianism. In the outcomes test, one lists the outcomes and evaluates the benefits and costs associated with each outcome. The right option is the outcome that yields the maximum benefit for the maximum number of people or stakeholders.

This test supports rational decision-making and logical reasoning. However, it requires one to know all the options and be able to evaluate the costs and benefits of each alternative quantitatively. This may be a challenging task. Qualitative parameters like goodwill, reputation, loss of community support, or even environmental damage may be difficult to quantify. There are methodologies for this test, but each has its assumptions and limitations.

Let's take the case of a beverage manufacturing company. The company faces negative publicity and reviews for using high sugar content in its products. In this scenario, the company could reduce sugar content, change its marketing campaigns, or stop production altogether. The best alternative would be the one that yields the maximum benefit for the company and its stakeholders. This includes employees, suppliers, customers, society, media, government, and so on. In this case, a transparent label, an open-minded acceptance of critique rather than a defensive approach, and a transition towards healthier offerings would yield maximum benefits.

3.4.3 Rights test

Using the rights test, one may analyze if the options from the list of alternatives violate anyone's rights. These rights may pertain to any living entity, including flora and fauna. For reference, one may access the fundamental rights per the constitution of where one belongs. Human rights may also be considered as a reference anywhere in the world. These include the right to life, liberty, education, freedom of speech, freedom from slavery, and others.

The rights test usually suggests an option that is universally applicable and acceptable; however, if constitutional rights differ across geographies, it may lead to contradictory choices. Let's consider the rights of different genders to childcare leave. In countries that still do not recognize gay marriage, the right option per human rights may conflict with the legal option. Further, in some cases, rights are proposed according to human viewpoints, not considering the perspectives of other species on the planet. For example, generally sustainable development is understood as meeting the needs of present generations without compromising the needs of future generations. This viewpoint is very human-centric.

For example, the rights test may be applied when the hiring policy is finalized by the HR department in a business. The policy should be designed in a way that recognizes human rights.

Further learning (link also available in Online Resources)
"Ethical Tests" https://bit.ly/3X2nWpU

3.4.4 Everybody test

This test lets one decide by questioning, "What if everybody picks the same option?" The chosen option should be safe even if everyone starts doing the same. When one is doubtful about the right choice, one may apply this test and assess the repercussions of this alternative if a large population follows it.

The test helps identify tasks and activities that benefit the organization or society. However, it will not encourage exceptional decisions that make a statement or defy the established fabric of society. Consider protests against minimum wages established by law. From the perspective of many stakeholders, it may not be suitable to choose from the "everybody test" lens in this case. It can lead to anarchy because stakeholders' interests usually coincide. Therefore, reaching a consensus through a win-win approach each time is practically impossible.

A clear example of the everybody test option could be coming late to work. An employee may feel "What difference would it make if I turned up late?" One will understand why coming late is wrong by imagining a workplace where everyone comes late to work. If all the employees start breaking the rules, the organization will not be able to function effectively.

3.4.5 Choices test

This test implies that when a decision is made, every stakeholder is aware of the choices and has a say in the decision. This is crucial for a company that strives to maximize stakeholder wealth.

The test's strength is that it considers multiple factors and perspectives, which is also a weakness since it may be challenging to reach a consensus when many parties are involved in decision-making.

An example of a choice test would be a stakeholder meeting while deciding whether a manufacturing plant should be located in a particular region. This decision shall affect the company shareholders, board of directors, managers and employees, community members in that region, the government, suppliers, etc. When the community is a marginalized stakeholder, the company must make an additional effort to acknowledge their viewpoint when choosing the plant location. This approach will be ethical and eventually beneficial for the company in the long run.

3.4.6 Justice test

As discussed in section 2.5 of Chapter Two, some ethical choices overlap with legal recourses while others do not. In the latter case, we may have options that are ethical but not legal or legal but not ethical. When ethical choices overlap with legal options, one can easily decide or distinguish between right and wrong. One can easily choose the option that is just and fair in the eyes of the law. Selecting the ethical choice this way comes under applying the justice test.

The strength of this test is that it is easy to apply since laws or regulations are already available to assess the right choice. The challenge, however, exists if one must identify the victim and the culprit. The essence of the final choice must be fair to all, and any partiality, influence, or inducement should not matter while making the decision.

An example of a justice test in a unique situation could be justice for the flora on the planet. In some countries, rivers have legal rights like humans. Thus, any discharge into the river by the business organization can be contested against by the river as a person. If the justice test is applied, by no means, does any company have the right to discharge harmful chemicals into rivers.

3.4.7 Character/Virtue test

This test is derived from the concept of virtue ethics. The application of this test tells one whether the outcome aligns with one's character or virtues. If I choose an option, does it match the person I want to become? If yes, it is the right choice for me.

The strength of this test is that it encourages integrity and enables an organization to live by the ideals it proposes and stands for. An example of this test would be if an organization strictly follows a zero-tolerance policy for corruption and never indulges in any activity that encourages corruption or related activities. The downside could be that idealism may become too challenging to implement for the organization, and they may have to bear the financial costs of choosing the right alternative.

Choosing right over wrong can be exhausting and confusing in a world of contradictions. The tests mentioned above may be used, one at a time or in combination with each other, to suggest a suitable alternative. The various tests for ethical decision-making explained in this section, have been summarized in Table 3.2 below:

Table 3.2	Overview of ethical decision-making tests		
Test Name	**Description**	**Strengths**	**Challenges**
Viral News Test	Considers if the decision would be acceptable if made public	Promotes societal values	May not consider minority viewpoints
Outcomes Test	Evaluates options based on maximum benefit for the maximum number of people	Supports rational decision-making	Difficult to quantify qualitative factors
Rights Test	Analyzes if the decision violates any fundamental rights	Ensures respect for universal rights	Legal rights may vary across regions
Everybody Test	Assesses if the decision would be safe if everyone chose the same option	Identifies beneficial tasks for society	May not encourage unique or exceptional decisions
Justice Test	Considers what is fair and just in the eyes of the law	Easy to apply with available regulations	Identifying the true victim and culprit can be challenging
Choices Test	Assesses if everyone affected by the decision has a say in the final choice	Encourages equity and justice for all	Difficult to reach a consensus in case of multiple stakeholders
Character Test	Aligns decision with one's character or virtues	Encourages organizational values	Subjective and restricted to the organization

Discussion Questions

1. Explain ethical dilemmas with an example.

2. Distinguish between teleological and deontological frameworks.

3. How can ethics be institutionalized in business organizations?

4. A firm has changed its packaging from red to green. A consultant advises the company to run a campaign that the company has committed to sustainability by changing its packaging color. Elaborate on applying viral tests to make the right decision in this situation.

5. Which "rights" are included when a manager evaluates decision choices using the rights test?

Chapter Summary

◆ Decision-making is a manager's primary job, and they must make efficient and effective decisions.

◆ Decisions faced by managers include ethical dilemmas involving different stakeholders or functional areas. However, the solution mainly lies at the intersection of areas.

◆ Organizational decision-making frameworks may be derived from teleological or deontological philosophies. These frameworks must be institutionalized for effective adoption and implementation.

◆ Different tests that can be used to make ethical choices when facing dilemmas are the viral test, outcomes test, rights test, everybody test, choices test, justice test, and character test.

Quiz

1. **According to Koontz and O'Donnell, which of the following is one of the primary functions of managers?**

   a. Innovation

   b. Direction

   c. Administration

   d. Office Management

2. **What is the essence of management, as per the discussion in the chapter?**

   a. Planning

   b. Decision-making

   c. Controlling

   d. Organizing

3. **Which of the following factors does NOT typically influence organizational decision-making criteria?**

   a. Legal considerations

   b. Ethical standards

   c. Social trends

   d. Personal preferences

4. **The "Utilitarian Model" of decision-making focuses on:**

   a. Maximizing individual rights

   b. Ensuring fairness and justice

   c. Achieving the greatest good for the greatest number

   d. Protecting stakeholder interests

5. **Which model of ethical decision-making prioritizes individual rights and freedoms?**
   a. Utilitarian model
   b. Rights model
   c. Justice model
   d. Care model

6. **The "Justice Model" in ethical decision-making is concerned with:**
   a. Fair distribution of benefits and burdens
   b. Maximizing overall happiness
   c. Upholding individual freedoms
   d. Promoting compassion and empathy

7. **Which of the following is NOT a step in the ethical decision-making process?**
   a. Identifying the ethical issue
   b. Generating alternatives
   c. Implementing a decision
   d. Ignoring stakeholder feedback

8. **The "Rights Model" in ethical decision-making emphasizes:**
   a. Consequential outcomes
   b. Fairness and equity
   c. Respect for individual rights
   d. Maximization of happiness

9. **Which model of ethical decision-making is most concerned with the fairness of outcomes?**

   a. Utilitarian model

   b. Rights model

   c. Justice model

   d. Care model

10. **Which ethical decision-making model would most likely emphasize empathy and relationships?**

    a. Utilitarian model

    b. Rights model

    c. Justice model

    d. Care model

Answers	1 – b	2 – b	3 – d	4 – c	5 – b
	6 – a	7 – d	8 – c	9 – c	10 – d

Chapter **4**

Corporate Social Responsibility

KEY LEARNING OBJECTIVES

- Explain the concept and evolution of CSR.
- Discuss the relationship between CSR and business ethics.
- Distinguish between strategic and non-strategic CSR.
- Describe the challenges and opportunities in the CSR domain.

This chapter offers a complete overview of the concept of Corporate Social Responsibility (CSR), and its relationship with business ethics. CSR is a widely used concept in the business and management literature. As a practice, it has existed since the advent of business. However, references in the literature to CSR started gaining prominence in the 1950s.[40]

---

40. Archie B. Carroll, "A History of Corporate Social Responsibility: Concepts and Practices," in *The Oxford Handbook of Corporate Social Responsibility*, eds. Andrew Crane, Dirk Matten, Abagail McWilliams, Jeremy Moon, and Donald S. Siegel (Oxford University Press, 2008), 19-46.

We delve into the evolution of CSR and the contradictions within its definitions. And explore the practical implementation of CSR. We also explain the difference between strategic and non-strategic approaches to CSR. Finally, challenges and opportunities are discussed to provide a complete picture.

4.1 Understanding CSR

CSR stands for corporate social responsibility. This term is widely used in the corporate world. CSR refers to the idea that business organizations must be responsible for their actions towards society. Since business organizations affect the lives of citizens in myriad ways, they must try to reduce negative externalities and create a positive impact.

Defining CSR is difficult, as businesses and researchers have interpreted it differently. Stobierski[41] defines CSR as the business's responsibility to the society in which it operates. According to Fordham and Robinson,[42] CSR can be linked to the stakeholder theory to explain that CSR contributions enable a firm to meet the needs of different stakeholders. Kotler and Lee[43] define CSR as the voluntary commitment of businesses to the community's well-being. According to the United Nations Industrial Development Organization, CSR is the concept by which companies integrate social and environmental concerns into their business decisions.[44]

Going by the above, one can conclude that no single definition summarizes all the characteristics of a company's

41. "Eye-opening Corporate Social Responsibility Statistics," *Harvard Business School Online*, accessed July 12, 2024, https://online.hbs.edu

42. A.E. Fordham and G. M. Robinson, "Mapping Meanings of Corporate Social Responsibility–An Australian Case Study," *International Journal of Corporate Social Responsibility*, no. 3 (2018): 1-20.

43. Philip Kotler and Nancy Lee, "Best of Breed: When It Comes to Gaining a Market Edge While Supporting a Social Cause, 'Corporate Social Marketing' Leads the Pack," *Social Marketing Quarterly* 11, no. 3-4 (2005): 91-103.

44. "What's CSR," *United Nations Industrial Development Organisation*, accessed July 12, 2024, https://www.unido.org

social responsibility. The meaning ranges from philanthropy to internalizing social and environmental criteria in business decisions. Although the meaning is interpreted differently, it is clear that all the meanings come under the purview of business ethics since the central idea of all CSR definitions is to promote purpose over profit in a business organization. The following subsections discuss the evolution of CSR, its relationship with ethics, CSR regulations, and best practices.

Further learning (link also available in Online Resources)
"The Social Responsibility of Business" https://bit.ly/3EPd887

4.2 Evolution of CSR

The concept of CSR was mostly written about during the mid-twentieth century.[45] While charity or integrating social and environmental concerns into business goals and practices are not new ideas, "CSR" was conceptualized a few decades ago.[46]

In 1953, Bowen discussed the idea that businesses and society are inextricably linked, and the former affects the latter and vice-versa in many ways.[47] Davis[48] linked CSR to religion. As each religion propagates a robust value system, CSR extends the need for a business to contribute to society and the environment.

In 1970, Friedman wrote that "the business of a business is to do business, without deception or fraud, within the rules of the

---

45. Archie B. Carroll, "A History of Corporate Social Responsibility: Concepts and Practices," in *The Oxford Handbook of Corporate Social Responsibility*, eds. Andrew Crane, Dirk Matten, Abagail McWilliams, Jeremy Moon, and Donald S. Siegel (Oxford University Press, 2008), 19-46.

46. Ritika Mahajan, "Corporate Social Responsibility in India: Revisiting Carroll's Pyramid and The Road Ahead," *Pacific Business Review International* 7, no. 9 (2015): 91-96.

47. Howard R. Bowen, *Social Responsibilities of the Businessman* (2013).

48. Keith Davis, "Understanding the Social Responsibility Puzzle." *Business Horizons* 10, no. 4 (1967): 45-50.

game."[49] According to the author, a business must focus on its core activities, yielding profit and leading to value creation. However, the latter part of the statement also emphasized the importance of remaining within the rules and regulations, and away from fraudulent activities. In other words, it implies abiding by ethical expectations and legal obligations.

In 1988, Freeman proposed the stakeholder theory.[50] We discussed this theory in section 1.5 of Chapter One, and its emphasis on business purpose and conduct for the benefit of stakeholders. According to this theory, CSR becomes significant from the viewpoint that the purpose of a business is to consider the interests of all stakeholders. The society and the environment are also included in the list of such stakeholders. Thus, societal development or environmental protection activities under CSR are aligned with the business purpose of maximizing stakeholder wealth. CSR is not anything extra the business must bear; it is part of the larger business goal.

A wide range of CSR definitions and ideas have been summarized over the years, effectively in Carroll's[51] CSR pyramid. According to Carroll, CSR responsibilities can be classified into economic, legal, ethical, and charitable; charity was replaced by philanthropy in a revised edition of the pyramid by Carroll in 1991.[52]

As per the CSR pyramid, the social responsibility of a business begins with fulfilling economic obligations. This includes providing a return on investment to shareholders, offering competitive salaries to employees, generating employment,

---

49. Milton Friedman, "A Friedman Doctrine: The Social Responsibility of Business is to Increase its Profits," *The New York Times*, September 13, 1970, https://www.nytimes.com

50. R. Edward Freeman, Daniel R. Gilbert, and Edward Hartman, "Values and the Foundations of Strategic Management," *Journal of Business Ethics* 7 (1988): 821-834.

51. Archie B. Carroll, "A Three-Dimensional Conceptual Model of Corporate Performance," *Academy of Management Review* 4, no. 4 (1979): 497-505.

52. Archie B. Carroll, "The Pyramid of Corporate Social Responsibility: Toward the Moral Management of Organizational Stakeholders," *Business Horizons* 34, no. 4 (1991): 39-48.

contributing to GDP, creating opportunities for supply chain partners, and so on.

The next level represents legal responsibility, which implies that the business must meet the requirements of the laws of the land. Legal obligations are not voluntary in nature. Every business must operate within the sphere of legal responsibility. However, in countries where breaking the law does not lead to strict penalties, where the enforcement mechanisms are weak, or corruption is rampant, abiding by the law appears to be a part of CSR.

The third level is ethical responsibility - choosing the right actions suited to the business context. While ethical responsibility seems voluntary, it may also be mandatory. For instance, in highly competitive markets, customer satisfaction becomes a mandate for the business to meet industry norms and benchmarks.

The final level of the CSR pyramid represents philanthropic responsibility. Initially, the term charity was used; it was then replaced by philanthropy. The latter is a more organized and continuous investment for social upliftment and progress.

Since the advent of organized business, business owners have made societal contributions. These contributions are intended to give back to the society where the business thrives. Specifically, it must not include contributions aimed at profit-making. However, social reputation and positive brand image are usually associated with such contributions. Philanthropy is also criticized in cases of greenwashing, wherein a business made through highly unsustainable technologies may contribute a part of the profit made in this way, to cancel the negative publicity.

In a paper by Carroll in 2016, the author revisited the pyramid and suggested that it must be looked at as a unified whole rather than in parts.[53] Some tensions and trade-offs are very naturally present when we combine different levels. Further, the pyramid can be used as a stakeholder engagement framework for practical

---

53. Archie B. Carroll, "Carroll's Pyramid of CSR: Taking Another Look," *International Journal of Corporate Social Responsibility* 1 (2016): 1-8.

purposes, with applications to different global contexts. The CSR pyramid by Carroll is shown below in Figure 4.1.

Figure 4.1   **CSR Pyramid Carroll (1991)**

Source: Caroll (2016)[54]

Having understood the evolution of CSR, one can conclude that ethics traverse all CSR levels. The next section describes the relationship between different CSR levels and business ethics.

4.3 Relationship Between CSR and Business Ethics

As we learned in section 4.2 above, according to Carroll,[55] ethics "permeate" all levels of CSR. To begin with, economic responsibility is the key to the survival and acceptance of business.

---

54. Carroll, "Carroll's Pyramid of CSR: Taking Another Look."
55. Carroll, "Carroll's Pyramid of CSR: Taking Another Look."

Society requires businesses to be economically viable to contribute through CSR. However, with increasing emphasis on sustainable development and business models, economic responsibility is not devoid of ethical considerations.

The surplus is important, but how the business made the surplus is equally important. In Eastern philosophy, this concept is described as *"shubh labh"* and is translated as "auspicious gain."[56] The purpose of business is not just to make a profit by all means but to generate an auspicious gain. Such gain is generated by integrating ethics in raising capital, budgeting that capital, operating the business, and earning a return on investment.

The second level, i.e. legal responsibility is called "codified ethics."[57] The regulators and society expect the business to be a law-abiding entity. The ethical practices expected by businesses are mentioned in the laws and regulations they are required to follow. The fundamental purpose of these regulations is to create a just and fair society with ethics inherent in spirit.

The third level is directly about ethics. As discussed in subsection 4.2 of this chapter, these ethics are reflected even in Friedman's proposition. Businesses must fulfill their core objective of making profits but not through unethical practices. Ethics may also be compulsions driven by competition.

The fourth level of philanthropy also integrates ethics. Giving back to society may be explained from a utilitarian, duty, or virtue perspective. From a utilitarian perspective, firms may engage in philanthropy to create a positive image that will increase brand equity, customer loyalty, supplier goodwill, and shareholder demand. Some firms may give back to society through philanthropy, considering it their duty. In contrast, others may engage in it to become known as organizations that care for their stakeholders, including society and the environment.

---

56. R. Garg and D. Saluja, "A Business Paradigm for Corporate Shubh–Labh: An Inquest Study," *Jindal Journal of Business Research* 6, no. 2 (2017): 146-154.
57. Garg and Saluja, "A Business Paradigm for Corporate Shubh–Labh: An Inquest Study."

The four levels of CSR and their integration with ethics, and examples, have been summarized in Table 4.1 below:

Table 4.1	**Integration of CSR and ethics**		
Level	**Description**	**Integration of Ethics**	**Example**
Economic Responsibility	Businesses must be economically viable for societal acceptance.	Profits should be made ethically (auspicious gain).	Ethical capital raising and fair pricing strategies
Legal Responsibility	Businesses must follow laws and regulations.	Compliance with labor laws and environmental standards	Paying fair wages and ensuring safe working conditions
Ethical Responsibility	Involves creating value ethically	Fairness and integrity in all stakeholder dealings	Addressing grievances and welfare concerns transparently
Philanthropic Responsibility	Giving back to society through various projects	Philanthropy to enhance brand image and societal welfare	Recycling projects and community training programs

To understand the relationship between CSR and business ethics better, let us take the example of a multinational corporation selling sportswear. From an economic viewpoint, the firm must generate profit to sustain itself. It must create a return for its shareholders, provide salaries to its employees at par with industry standards, pay suppliers their dues on time, and generate a return for its investors. While meeting these obligations, it must choose a path devoid of financial fraud, misrepresentation, fabrication, or falsification.

While this company produces sportswear, it must follow all legal requirements. For instance, labor must be paid minimum wages, and their working conditions must meet the prescribed requirements. The technology and waste disposal must be sustainable, per government mandates.

The third level implies that the firm must pay attention to stakeholders' ethical matters. These include matters such as addressing customer grievances, employee welfare concerns, community problems in adjoining areas, supplier concerns, etc. As per the fourth level, the firm may engage in long-term, philanthropic projects like recycling shoes or training community members to enable them to seek decent livelihoods. Ethics forms the essence of running a business in all these examples and instances. Thus, CSR is inextricably linked to business ethics.

4.4 Strategic and Non-Strategic CSR

From a business perspective, CSR can be classified as strategic and non-strategic. The term strategic CSR was given by Porter and Kramer in Harvard Business Review.[58] Strategic CSR was later termed as the concept of "Creation of Shared Value" by the authors in a paper published in 2011.[59] Shared Value Creation refers to business organizations' simultaneous pursuit of economic and social value.[60] In the authors' words - businesses as businesses, and not as charitable organizations can be more effective in providing solutions to the fiercest challenges of the world.

---

58. Mark R. Kramer and Michael E. Porter, "Strategy and Society: The Link Between Competitive Advantage and Corporate Social Responsibility," *Harvard Business Review* 84, no. 12 (2006): 78-92.

59. Mark R. Kramer and Marc W. Pfitzer, "The Ecosystem of Shared Value," *Harvard Business Review* 94, no. 10 (2016): 80-89.

60. Mark R. Kramer and Michael E. Porter. *Creating Shared Value.* Boston, MA, USA: FSG, 2011.

In this context, a firm can identify opportunities to develop products that offer useful services to society and generate profits. The firm can also generate shared value by re-evaluating its value chains and enabling the development of the community in which the business operates. By engaging in these activities, a business can make a social impact and run a profitable venture. However, this notion may be critiqued as capitalistic or transactional.

The other type, non-strategic CSR, is when the business organization undertakes socially responsible initiatives without the intention of making a profit. Anything that contributes to profit-making is not considered as CSR. For example, proponents of this school of thought argue that employee welfare expenditures should not be classified as CSR. While such spending benefits the company, it does not provide direct advantages to society.

In the context of the United Nations, CSR initiatives are undertaken by companies voluntarily to contribute to society and the environment.[61] Camilleri[62] critically appraises the United States of America (USA) government policies for CSR and describes the attributes of American firms engaged in CSR. However, there are some countries, where selected firms meeting the cut-off criteria of profit, net worth, or revenue are mandated to contribute to CSR activities. Further, such activities must not create any economic benefit for the firm.

Following Table 4.2 offers a comparison view of strategic and non-strategic CSR with examples and criticism.

61. "United Nations Industrial Development Organization," accessed July 12, 2024, https://www.unido.org

62. Mark A. Camilleri, "The Integrated Reporting of Financial, Social and Sustainability Capitals: A Critical Review and Appraisal," *International Journal of Sustainable Society* 9, no. 4 (2017): 311-326.

Table 4.2	Strategic and non-strategic CSR	
Aspect	**Strategic CSR (Creation of Shared Value)**	**Non-Strategic CSR**
Definition	CSR activities that create both economic and social value for the business	CSR activities are undertaken purely for social and environmental benefits, without direct profit motives
Coined By	Porter and Kramer (2006[63]) later expanded in 2011[64]	Not specifically attributed to a single originator
Examples	Developing socially valuable products and services; re-evaluating value chains for social impact; community development initiatives	Community health camps; scholarships for underprivileged children; plantation drives
Criticism	Viewed as capitalistic or transactional	Sometimes criticized for lack of integration with core business strategy

4.5 CSR: Opportunities and Challenges

CSR is an evolving concept. Organizations across the globe have embraced CSR in various ways. There are many benefits associated with CSR investments by companies. These relate to brand equity, customer perception, competitive advantage, supplier relationships, civil society support, community engagement, and long-term financial sustainability. These benefits generate opportunities for firms to utilize CSR to create a net

63. Mark R. Kramer and Michael E. Porter, "Strategy and Society: The Link Between Competitive Advantage and Corporate Social Responsibility," Harvard Business Review 84, no. 12 (2006): 78-92.

64. Mark R. Kramer and Michael E. Porter. *Creating Shared Value*. Boston, MA, USA: FSG, 2011.

positive impact for themselves and the society. However, there are challenges too. Some of these challenges are described ahead.

First, CSR is a voluntary commitment. Thus, it requires an intent to give back to the society. In a highly competitive environment, such voluntary commitments can make it challenging to balance profitability and responsibility. Second, stakeholder awareness is increasing, and information is widely and quickly circulated to a large audience through social media. Thus, implementing CSR initiatives is challenging because stakeholders demand transparency and question whether the firm's efforts are genuine or merely a form of greenwashing. Earning credibility from the stakeholders' point of view is an achievement.

Third, although CSR is widely practiced, not all firms undertake CSR impact assessment. While it is essential to undertake CSR projects for social objectives, assessing the impact of such projects is critical to identify best practices and challenges. Legally, very few regulations emphasize CSR impact assessment. There is also lack of standardized methodologies and the difficulty of assessing qualitative transformation enabled by CSR activities. Fourth, regulatory compliance can be highly expensive for some organizations, making it difficult for them to voluntarily commit to CSR beyond those requirements.

Fifth, the global agenda for sustainable development has pressured businesses to adopt responsible practices. This includes investments in greener technologies and circular economy initiatives emphasizing recycling, reducing, reusing, and committing to carbon emission reductions. In such a scenario, CSR may take a backseat as the focus shifts from contributing a percentage of profits to society, to the core operations leading to profit-making.

Further learning (link also available in Online Resources)
"The Era of CSR is Ending" https://bit.ly/4aZ0gbM

Sixth, CSR demands resource allocation including time, effort, and money. Not all firms may be interested in such allocation or they may be skeptical about CSR benefits. Seventh, short-term or single intervention-based initiatives hardly create any long-term impacts. CSR demands a long-term commitment to creating a sustainable impact.

Eighth, stakeholders may not support CSR initiatives. For instance, shareholders may require a return on investment in the short run, which may decrease if the firm engages in CSR. Similarly, customers may prefer better product quality over cause-related charity. Ninth, designing CSR interventions requires particular expertise and experience. Finding people suitable for the role may be challenging. Finally, there are very few models of successful CSR investment. What works and what does not work needs more research.

While these challenges exist, opportunities are also prevalent. In the changing narrative of corporate purpose, we are now moving towards corporate sustainability rather than corporate philanthropy. The next chapter sheds more light on corporate philanthropy and its relationship with business ethics.

Discussion Questions

1. Discuss the viewpoints of Friedman and Freeman on CSR.

2. Distinguish between strategic and non-strategic CSR. Which is a better approach?

3. How is the economic level of Carroll's CSR Pyramid linked to business ethics?

4. Are there any pitfalls of philanthropy? Explain.

5. The Era of CSR is ending. Critically review the statement and explain your viewpoint.

Chapter Summary

◆ CSR is a widely used concept in the corporate sector, but there are many definitions and interpretations.

◆ Carroll's Pyramid summarizes different aspects of CSR into four levels - economic, legal, ethical, and philanthropic. Ethics traverse all levels of CSR. The pyramid also reflects the application of stakeholder theory.

◆ Strategic CSR is the simultaneous pursuit of economic and social value, while non-strategic CSR is undertaken only for societal benefit.

◆ The downside of CSR is that most of the funds are spent in a few priority areas based on management's discretion. CSR requires long-term commitment and balancing both short-term and long-term profitability, to be beneficial.

Quiz

1. **What is the primary concept behind Corporate Social Responsibility (CSR)?**
   a. Maximizing profits at all costs
   b. Maintaining a high market share
   c. Being responsible for the impact of business actions on society
   d. Minimizing operational costs

2. **According to Kotler and Lee (2005), CSR is defined as:**
   a. A legal obligation to follow regulations
   b. The business's responsibility to the community's well-being
   c. A strategy to increase market share
   d. The mandatory allocation of resources for environmental causes

3. **Which organization/ author defines CSR as integrating social and environmental concerns into business decisions?**
   a. Stobierski
   b. United Nations Industrial Development Organization
   c. Fordham and Robinson
   d. Kotler and Lee

4. **What does the term philanthropy in CSR refer to according to Carroll (1991)?**
   a. Compliance with legal standards
   b. Voluntary contributions to societal well-being
   c. Generating profits for shareholders
   d. Meeting ethical standards

5. **In which year did Bowen discuss the connection between businesses and society?**
   a. 1953
   b. 1970
   c. 1988
   d. 2008

6. **Who linked CSR to religion in 1967?**
   a. Milton Friedman
   b. Carroll
   c. Davis
   d. Freeman

7. **What was the central argument of Milton Friedman's 1970 paper regarding CSR?**
   a. Businesses should focus on creating social value above profits.
   b. The primary business function is to maximize profit within legal boundaries.
   c. CSR is a mandatory requirement for all businesses.
   d. Businesses should avoid legal compliance.

8. **Who proposed the stakeholder theory, which emphasizes considering the interests of all stakeholders in CSR?**

    a. Carroll

    b. Friedman

    c. Freeman

    d. Kotler

9. **How do ethics relate to the levels of the CSR pyramid given by Carroll?**

    a. Ethics are irrelevant to CSR levels.

    b. Ethics permeate all levels of CSR.

    c. Ethics apply only to legal responsibilities.

    d. Ethics are only important in philanthropic activities.

10. **What is the term used to describe the integration of ethical practices in generating profits?**

    a. Ethical Capital

    b. Philanthropy

    c. Legal Compliance

    d. Auspicious Gain

Answers	1 – c	2 – b	3 – b	4 – b	5 – a
	6 – c	7 – b	8 – c	9 – b	10 – d

Chapter 5

Sustainability and Ethical Business Practices

> ### KEY LEARNING OBJECTIVES
>
> - Explain the concept of sustainable development and sustainability.
> - Understand the relationship between sustainability and business ethics.
> - Identify and discuss sustainable business models and practices.
> - Use and evaluate different business reports for ethical decision-making.
> - Compare challenges and global perspectives on sustainability.

This chapter is a complete guide to understanding the concept of business sustainability and its role in promoting ethics in businesses. We shall explore the meaning of sustainability, its evolution and current status in the business world. We'll also learn about various sustainable business models and practices. This will help us understand how they relate to the idea of an ethical business. Finally, different reporting formats for disclosing sustainability impacts are explained. This is followed by associated challenges and a global outlook.

5.1 Understanding Sustainability

In 1987, the World Commission on Environment and Development chaired by the Norwegian Prime Minister, Gro Harlem Brundtland released the Brundtland Commission Report.[65] This report propounded the widely used definition of sustainable development based on inter-generational equity.

Since the late 1980s, there has been a growing emphasis on decoupling growth and development from environmental and social inequality.[66] In 2000, United Nations member nations adopted eight Millennium Development Goals (MDGs) to improve people's lives by committing to fight against poverty, hunger, environmental degradation, discrimination, and so on. In 2015, the MDGs were replaced by the Sustainable Development Goals (SDGs).[67]

As mentioned in Chapter One, the SDGs were adopted by United Nations member states and they comprise 169 targets. These targets aim to transition countries towards development that is socially and environmentally sustainable.[68] The goals aim at ending poverty and hunger and ensuring peace and prosperity for all. The SDGs, directed toward sustainable development, can only be achieved by the combined efforts of different stakeholders.

---

65. "Brundtland Commission Report," World Commission for Sustainable Development, accessed July 12, 2024, https://sustainabledevelopment.un.org

66. Juan Infante-Amate, Emiliano Travieso, and Eduardo Aguilera, "Unsustainable prosperity? Decoupling wellbeing, economic growth, and greenhouse gas emissions over the past 150 years," *World Development* 184 (2024): 106754.

67. "Sustainable Development Goals," accessed July 26, 2024, https://sdgs.un.org

68. "Sustainable Development Goals (SDGs) (Agenda 2030)," United Nations, accessed July 12, 2024, https://sdgs.un.org

Post-2015, governments at national and local levels, implemented policies driving such changes. Because of their competencies, resources, and scales, businesses are important stakeholders that can contribute to building a sustainable world. Thus, business sustainability started getting traction due to policies and increasing levels of stakeholder awareness.

In simple words, business sustainability refers to considering social and environmental impacts while maximizing profit-making. It is also known as the "Triple Bottom Line" approach.[69] This approach means that while companies must prioritize economic gains they should also evaluate the social and environmental consequences of their decisions and operations. Thus, sustainability is a three-dimensional approach to governing and managing a business organization.

Although the concepts of Ethics, CSR, and Sustainability are interconnected, they have different meanings. Let's look at the difference between them, with examples in Table 5.1 below:

Table 5.1	Difference between ethics, CSR, and sustainability

Aspect	Definition	Example
Ethics	Principles of right and wrong conduct, guiding individual and organizational behavior	A company adheres to fair labor practices. It ensures equal pay and opportunities for all employees regardless of gender, ethnicity, or background.
CSR	The company's responsibility to society and the environment often includes voluntary actions beyond legal requirements.	A company invests in community development projects such as building schools or providing clean water access to underprivileged communities.

---

69. John Elkington, "The Triple Bottom Line," in *Environmental Management: Readings and Cases*, (1997), 49-66.

Aspect	Definition	Example
Sustainability	Meeting present needs without compromising future generations' ability to meet their needs	Implementing renewable energy sources and sustainable waste management practices reduces environmental impact. It ensures long-term resource availability.

Business sustainability is challenging to implement because an ecosystem needs to exist. Suppliers, investors, and customers must all work in tandem with the business. Transitioning from a linear to a circular economy helps promote sustainability.

In a circular economy, reusing, recycling, reducing, rethinking, and redesigning principles are employed to provide sustainable goods and services. We will discuss these principles in depth in section 5.3.

However, when it comes to sustainability in business, there are challenges related to leadership and intent, financial constraints and investor preferences, resources and business acumen, government support, and customer demands. Slowly and steadily, businesses are treading this path, and governments are also making policy amendments.

For instance, changes in the menu of fast-food joints, carbon footprint disclosures, and a reduction in emission targets by multinational corporations are some examples of changes toward business sustainability. Other examples include community engagement and development efforts by industry associations, inclusion of environment and social criteria by investors, and promotion of symbiotic relationships amongst industries by the government.

Further learning (link also available in Online Resources)
"Ray Anderson: The Business Logic of Sustainability"
https://bit.ly/42R3YlJ

The next section explains the relationship between sustainability and business ethics.

5.2 Relationship Between Sustainability and Business Ethics

A sustainable business is also known as a green business, corporate citizenship, and responsible business. CSR, as discussed in Chapter Four, is about allocating a portion of the profit towards socially responsible activities. In contrast, sustainability is about healthier technologies and methodologies employed in making a profit.

From an ethical standpoint, sustainability aims to maximize the value created by the firm for stakeholders. Along with customers, suppliers, and employees, society and the environment are also stakeholders. Thus, the essence of sustainability is ethical.

For example, a business organization faces backlash from the local public regarding a new project. In this case, the business must engage with the community to understand their problems and find a value-maximizing solution for all the affected parties. A sustainable business would proactively engage with the community and support it. From an ethical standpoint, be it from a utilitarian or duty perspective, society will view a firm that supports the community as ethical.

In another example, a beverage manufacturing firm plans to launch an environmentally sustainable, new product. The packaging team has been asked to assess various alternatives available in the market to find the one that helps the firm balance economic, social, and environmental aspects. From the sustainability lens, the firm invests in new packaging technology that uses bamboo rather than plastic because it is not harmful like plastic is, to the environment. This technology supports farmers and targets eco-conscious consumers.

The choice to adopt new packaging will require the firm to incur financial costs. However, in the long run, it will be advantageous to the firm as there will be benefits from government subsidies and increased prices borne by niche market consumers. The firm shall also save on costs by adapting to changes that may be mandated by regulators in the future. Economies of scale over time shall also yield higher returns to the firm. From an ethical viewpoint, considering the utilitarian perspective, investing in sustainability is the right choice because the firm gains in multiple ways in the long term.

5.3 Principles of a Sustainable Business

There are different ways to classify sustainability-centric business strategies. One of the primary methods is based on circular economy principles.[70] The categorization of these principles is discussed ahead.

The first circular economy principle is "recycling." A business organization may use recycling as a core competency in its business model or utilize it to transition toward sustainability. For example, a firm that recycles textile waste to sell bags is utilizing the principle as its core competency. Another example is a cosmetics company that recycles plastic shampoo bottles, that it collects from the market. They claim they recycle more plastic than they use and declare themselves plastic-negative.

"Reusing" is the second principle. Companies engaged in rental car business or wedding gown rentals may be considered as businesses utilizing "reusing" as the key sustainability strategy in their business model. Another example is a company that uses old tires to create play areas for children and cafeterias. These businesses are offering products as services and contributing towards building a shared economy. However, some firms may reuse certain parts of their products rather than rely on reusing them as the core business model.

---

70. Anne P. Velenturf and Peter Purnell, "Principles for a Sustainable Circular Economy," *Sustainable Production and Consumption*, no. 27 (2021): 1437-1457.

The third circular economy principle is "reducing." Reducing refers to ensuring a decrease in the consumption of resources. One example of reducing is a carpet tile manufacturing company, "Interface," that has drastically reduced its energy and water consumption to build a sustainable business model over the years. The company has solidified its position as a first mover in the sustainability domain, which has greatly strengthened its brand image. Reduction helps in the optimal utilization of resources. It inculcates principles of lean thinking and efficiency. Many business organizations have committed to reducing resource consumption and emissions by publicly declaring their targets.

"Rethinking" is the fourth principle of the circular economy approach. According to this principle, rethinking can enable businesses to integrate sustainability into their operations. For instance, solar panels in developing countries have slowly started becoming widely accepted by businesses. This is because of the "Operating Expenses (OPEX)" model, which does not require one to pay for capital expenditure.[71] One can pay the operating expenditure, and a third party, say a solar company, provides the panel on lease. By rethinking their business model, businesses could move towards renewable energy consumption.

"Redesigning" is the final principle. This principle is focused on the smart designing of products and services. Designing for sustainability is important if we want to build sustainable products. For instance, a product not built to be recycled easily would end up in a landfill. Take an example of a tetra pack. A tetra pack has layers of different materials, which need sophisticated technology to be separated and recycled. Thus, if we want to recycle our packaging materials easily, we must design them thoughtfully and innovatively.

The correlating ethical issues concerning these sustainability principles have been outlined below in Table 5.2 below:

---

71. "OPEX Model," accessed July 12, 2024, https://www.savills.in

Table 5.2 **Principles of sustainability and related ethical issues**

Principle	Meaning	Example	Ethical Issue
Recycling	Incorporating materials' reuse into business operations reduces waste and promotes sustainability.	A firm that recycles textile waste to create and sell bags	Ensuring transparent recycling practices are followed to avoid greenwashing or misleading claims.
Reusing	Utilizing products or materials multiple times in their original form or repurposed form, extends their lifecycle.	A company repurposing old tires to create play areas and cafeterias	Ensuring proper quality and safety standards are maintained when reusing materials to avoid negative impact on consumers.
Reducing	Minimizing resource consumption and waste generation through efficiency improvements and optimization of processes	Carpet tile manufacturer, "Interface" reducing energy and water consumption to build a sustainable business model	Balancing the need for resource efficiency with potential impacts on product quality, production costs, and employee welfare
Rethinking	Challenging traditional business models and practices to integrate sustainability principles, often through innovative approaches and alternative technologies	Adoption of solar panels in developing countries through an OPEX model; leasing panels rather than upfront purchase	Here, addressing potential issues of equity and access to sustainable technologies is key. This ensures benefits are distributed fairly across communities.

Principle	Meaning	Example	Ethical Issue
Redesigning	Incorporating sustainability into the design of products and services to minimize environmental impact	Designing packaging materials for easy recycling	Balancing sustainability with product functionality, consumer preferences, and cost considerations

5.4 Sustainability Reporting and Disclosures

As learned in the preceding section 5.3, sustainable business models and strategies aim to optimize resource utilization. Hence, the decisions driving businesses towards sustainability are inherently ethical. For stakeholders, it is difficult to understand and measure sustainability. Hence, business organizations must adhere to disclosures related to sustainability and release this data in the form of a report.

Different business organizations use different formats to prepare sustainability reports. The major types and purposes of these reports are outlined in Table 5.3 below:

Table 5.3 **Types of sustainability reports[72]**

Type of Report	Explanation
Annual Financial Report	Details a company's financial performance through financial statements, disclosures of past achievements, and future plans to inform stakeholders
Integrated Sustainability Report[73]	Combines financial and non-financial data regarding a company's financial, manufacturing, intellectual, human, social, and natural capital performance

---

72. "Types of Sustainability Reporting," accessed July 12, 2024, https://eka1.com
73. "Integrated Reporting," accessed July 12, 2024, https://integratedreporting.ifrs.org

Type of Report	Explanation
Social Responsibility Report[74]	Reporting CSR budgets, committees, projects, activities, governance, and impacts
Global Reporting Initiative (GRI) Report[75]	Reporting material issues, economic, social, and environmental impacts, and stakeholder engagement process
Carbon Disclosure Project (CDP) Report[76]	Reports greenhouse gas emissions and climate-related impacts of a company based on the Carbon Disclosure Project framework
Task Force on Climate-related Financial Disclosures (TCFD) Report[77]	Provides disclosures on climate-related financial risks and opportunities in accordance with the TCFD guidelines and recommendations
Sustainability Accounting Standards Board (SASB) Report[78]	Reports financial material sustainability issues, concerns, and disclosures for the investors
International Financial Reporting Standards (IFRS) Report[79]	Integrates financial and sustainability reporting in accordance with international financial reporting standards

Annual reports, presenting the financial performance of companies are publicly available for public limited companies. Sustainability reports on the other hand, include disclosures related to the social and environmental impacts of business operations. These reports are also known as non-financial reports, corporate citizenship reports, business responsibility reports, and integrated sustainability reports.

---

74. "Social Responsibility Report," accessed July 12, 2024, https://online.hbs.edu

75. "Global Reporting Initiative," accessed July 12, 2024, https://www.globalreporting.org

76. "Carbon Disclosure Project," accessed July 12, 2024, https://www.cdp.net

77. "Task Force on Climate-related Financial Disclosures (TCFD) Report," accessed July 12, 2024, https://www.fsb-tcfd.org

78. "Sustainability Accounting Standards Board (SASB) Report," accessed July 12, 2024, https://sasb.ifrs.org

79. "International Financial Reporting Standards," accessed July 26 2024, https://www.ifrs.org

Various frameworks are employed to create comprehensive sustainability reports. The Global Reporting Initiative (GRI) Standards are most widely used for sustainability reporting. These standards include universal, sector, and topic standards to disclose general information. They also include stakeholder engagement, materiality analysis, reporting principles, and economic, social, and environmental impacts. Other frameworks include the CDP report, the TCFD report, the SASB report, and the IFRS report.

In a social responsibility report, the critical information is related to CSR. These reports may include CSR projects, locations, budgets, committees, governance, and impacts. Some companies combine CSR data in an annual or sustainability report, while others may issue a standalone social responsibility report.

Companies may also report financial and non-financial data together in an integrated report. In these reports, companies track changes/increments in six types of capital as defined by the International Integrated Reporting Council. They are financial, manufacturing, human, intellectual, social, and natural capital.

Many governments are mandating such reports to hold companies accountable for their impacts. These reports are also being demanded by investors to evaluate the sustainability of projects.

5.5 Challenges and the Way Ahead

Companies face many challenges when it comes to building and running a sustainable business. Some of these challenges are discussed below:

Leadership

The first challenge is leadership. Sustainability may be "top-down" or "bottom-top" driven. However, there is a critical need for leaders who understand, accept, and execute what it takes to build a sustainable organization. Most companies known in this domain, like Interface or Patagonia, have been backed by the vision of strong leaders.

These leaders are known to have fought against all odds to build profitable, socially responsible, and environmentally accountable companies. There is a dearth of leaders with such vision, conviction, and belief. Building a sustainable organization requires courage and meticulous effort, especially amid the fierce competition, and global, economic, and political challenges.

Greenwashing

The second challenge is related to greenwashing.[80] Since going green has become a mandate, and there is a lot of media coverage and social media support for green initiatives, some companies indulge in greenwashing. This refers to malpractices of cheating customers by either hiding or disclosing information in a way that appears to be sustainable, but it is not.

For instance, the company prefers to utilize funds to advertise and brand itself as green or sustainable rather than investing in better technology that reduces harmful environmental impacts. In another case, a company may shift to green color packaging rather than substantially changing its offerings to make the customers feel that they are green or environmentally friendly.

Lack of framework or index

The third challenge pertains to a lack of framework, tool, or index to measure sustainability. Many sustainability reports run into hundreds of pages. Not all stakeholders understand the frameworks and the disclosures. While they may be able to browse the report, they may not understand the reality of the company's sustainability projects. This is true, especially for vulnerable and marginalized stakeholders.

---

80. S.V. de Freitas Netto, M. F. F. Sobral, A. R. B. Ribeiro, and G. R. D. L. Soares, "Concepts and Forms of Greenwashing: A Systematic Review," *Environmental Sciences Europe*, no. 32 (2020): 1-12.

There is also the lack of a unified framework for reporting. In some cases, the same company may use a different approach or format for sustainability reporting each year. Additionally, different companies within the same industry often employ varying frameworks. Thus, global comparisons of sustainability standards, within and among companies or industries, are very challenging to make.

Non-availability of sustainable business models

The non-availability of business models or ecosystems supporting sustainable practices also poses a challenge. To begin with, there are very few case studies of companies that have been able to internalize and use the idea of sustainability to offer products and services useful for society and the environment. Most templates available in the market do not provide much information to companies struggling to balance economic gains with social and environmental impacts. There is also a lack of examples for companies striving to adopt sustainable practices and assess the impact.

Insufficient stakeholder support

Finally, while companies are always considered villains in the capitalist economy, sometimes they cannot garner enough support from key stakeholders, even if the governance or management team is keen on promoting sustainability. Unless suppliers integrate sustainability across the supply chain, government provides financial and regulatory support, customers demand sustainable products, and employees prefer to work in sustainable companies, the transition to sustainable business organizations is extremely challenging. While customers indicate an intention to buy sustainable products, they may not. It takes a complete ecosystem to build a sustainable organization.

While these challenges exist, sustainability is paramount for the planet›s future. Business organizations have a responsibility towards the environment and society. While CSR is driven by regulatory and organizational mandates, sustainability, on the other hand, is at the heart of key business decisions. The latter involves critical decisions that impact the environment and quality of life on this planet.

Investing in renewable energy, community engagement, selection of suppliers after screening for environmental criteria, assessing sustainability impacts, and promoting green products are some of the key areas of business sustainability. Thus, despite the challenges, sustainability must drive the future of business organizations. The next chapter focuses on the role of leaders and top management in building such sustainable, ethical organizations.

Further learning (link also available in Online Resources)
"Steve Howard: Let's Go All-In Selling Sustainability"
https://bit.ly/3CF6zoh

Discussion Questions

1. How is sustainability different from sustainable development? Explain.

2. What is the relationship between sustainability and business ethics? Discuss.

3. If a company sells a product as a service to its customers, who use it for a fixed duration rather than owning the product, would the company business model fall in the category of a sustainable business? Discuss with the help of an example.

4. What are the key principles of sustainable business models?

5. Why is non-financial reporting important? How will it impact the future of reporting?

Chapter Summary

◆ Sustainability is an organizational concept, while sustainable development is a macro-level concept.

◆ Sustainability refers to internalizing concern for society and the environment in business decision-making. On the other hand, sustainable development aims to utilize economic resources in a way that does not compromise the needs of future generations.

◆ Business ethics are present throughout the concept of sustainability because they aim to protect and promote the interests of society and the environment. From a duty and a utilitarian perspective, sustainability aligns with ethics.

◆ The fundamental sustainable business principles are reusing, recycling, reducing, rethinking, and redesigning.

◆ The future of reporting is the integration of financial and non-financial disclosures. GRI Standards are the most widely used sustainability reporting standards.

◆ Greenwashing is a critical challenge in business sustainability. The lack of unified framework and tools for measuring sustainability is also a significant issue.

◆ The future of business lies in embracing sustainability, as it is critical to save the planet. Businesses, with their scale and resources, can make a significant impact by protecting the environment and society.

Quiz

1. **How many Sustainable Development Goals (SDGs) were adopted by United Nations member states in 2015?**
   a. 12
   b. 15
   c. 17
   d. 20

2. **What does the "Triple Bottom Line" approach refer to?**
   a. Focusing on economic gains only
   b. Internalizing societal and environmental concerns in business decision-making
   c. Balancing economic, social, and environmental considerations
   d. Concentrating solely on social impacts

3. **Which principle of sustainability focuses on minimizing resource consumption and waste generation?**
   a. Reusing
   b. Recycling
   c. Reducing
   d. Redesigning

4. **What is the primary aim of sustainability reporting?**
   a. To report financial performance only
   b. To provide data on social and environmental impacts
   c. To evaluate employee performance
   d. To highlight profit margins

5. **Which report focuses exclusively on disclosing greenhouse gas emissions?**

    a. Global Reporting Initiative (GRI) Report

    b. Task Force on Climate-related Financial Disclosures (TCFD) Report

    c. Carbon Disclosure Project (CDP) Report

    d. Social Responsibility Report

6. **What does the principle of reusing involve?**

    a. Using materials multiple times in their original form or repurposed form

    b. Reducing resource consumption

    c. Integrating sustainability into design

    d. Reprocessing waste materials

7. **Which sustainability report combines financial and non-financial data?**

    a. Annual Financial Report

    b. Integrated Sustainability Report

    c. Social Responsibility Report

    d. Sustainability Accounting Standards Board (SASB) Report

8. **Which of these indicators is an example of non-financial data?**

    a. Profit before tax

    b. Depreciation

    c. Recycled water

    d. Amortization

9. **Which company is mentioned as an example of a first-mover in leadership for sustainability?**

    a. Microsoft

    b. Interface

    c. Google

    d. Amazon

10. **Which principle of circular economy involves challenging traditional business models through innovative approaches?**

    a. Recycling

    b. Rethinking

    c. Reducing

    d. Reusing

Answers	1 – c	2 – c	3 – c	4 – b	5 – c
	6 – a	7 – b	8 – c	9 – b	10 – b

This page is intentionally left blank

Chapter 6

Leadership and Corporate Governance

KEY LEARNING OBJECTIVES

- Explain the role of leaders and leadership theories in sustaining an ethical organization.

- Evaluate the best practices, challenges, and leadership opportunities.

- Describe the meaning and role of corporate governance in business ethics.

- Analyze governance-related best practices for ethical organizations.

This chapter offers insight into leadership and governance practices for building an ethical organization. It discusses the role of leaders and governing bodies in implementing ethics. The association between leadership and ethics has been demonstrated with widely known leadership theories. They include trait, behavioral, and contingency theories. We will also discuss the difference between transactional and transformational leadership styles from an ethical perspective.

The following sections will explain the challenges, opportunities, and best practices of ethical leadership and corporate governance in businesses. The chapter also covers the meaning and role of corporate governance in building an ethical organization. Through strategic decision-making, governance bodies establish ethical codes of conduct and policies. This supports them in dealing with deviations from these ethics.

6.1 Introduction

An organization's decision to pursue ethics through frameworks, codes of conduct, other policies, and rules is the prerogative of its leadership and top management. Thus, understanding the need for leadership, as well as the governance structure and practices used to build and nurture an ethical organization is essential. This chapter covers these details.

There are two approaches to management: top-down and bottom-up.[81] In the former approach, business decisions are made at the top management level and communicated down the hierarchy. For instance, the top management may decide whether an ethical compliance officer will be appointed to the organization.

Some decisions may flow from the board of governors as undisputable compliances. Examples include setting up an ethics department, reporting disclosures, undergoing mandatory impact assessment in projects, and establishing a vision, mission, and clear guidelines for implementing ethics.

In the bottom-up approach, decisions are stimulated by voices at the level of employees, which then reach top management. For example, employees may bring to the top management's notice that a vendor disposes of hazardous waste in water bodies. Consequently, looking at the supply chain impacts, the company

---

81. Paul A. Sabatier, "Top-down and Bottom-up Approaches to Implementation Research," in *Policy Process* (Routledge, 2014), 272-295.

must take some action against the empanelment of this vendor in the company's list of suppliers.

At the same time, some ethical concerns may be voiced by field workers to promote a fair, transparent, and ethical culture in the organization. Examples may include employee compensation policies, community engagement strategies, vendor selection criteria, media management methods, etc.

Both top-down and bottom-up approaches function when it comes to formulating, implementing, and evaluating ethical policies and decisions. And ethical decisions can be driven through either approach. However, the support of top management and governance bodies is critical to achieving measurable outcomes. The following sections discuss cases, best practices, opportunities, and challenges for leaders and governing boards to nurture ethical organizations.

6.2 Role of Leadership in an Ethical Organization

A leader leads from the front. An ethical leader is expected to demonstrate ethical behavior, live a life upholding ethical values dear to the firm, and expend efforts to build a culture of ethical decision-making. Corporate leadership has been researched for a long time by organizational behavior theorists and practitioners.

Majorly from the point of view of whether leaders are made or born, there are trait, behavioral, and contingency theories (Watson, 1913[82]; Pavlov, 1927[83]; Skinner, 1938[84]; Mischel, 1968[85]).

82. John B. Watson, "Psychology as the Behaviorist Views It," *Psychological Review* 20, no. 2 (1913): 158-177. https://doi.org/10.1037/h0074428

83. Ivan P. Pavlov, *Conditioned Reflexes: An Investigation of the Physiological Activity of the Cerebral Cortex* (Oxford University Press, 1927).

84. B. F. Skinner, *The Behavior of Organisms: An Experimental Analysis* (New York: Appleton-Century, 1938).

85. Walter Mischell. *Personality and Assessment* (New York: Wiley, 1968).

Figure 6.1   Leadership theories

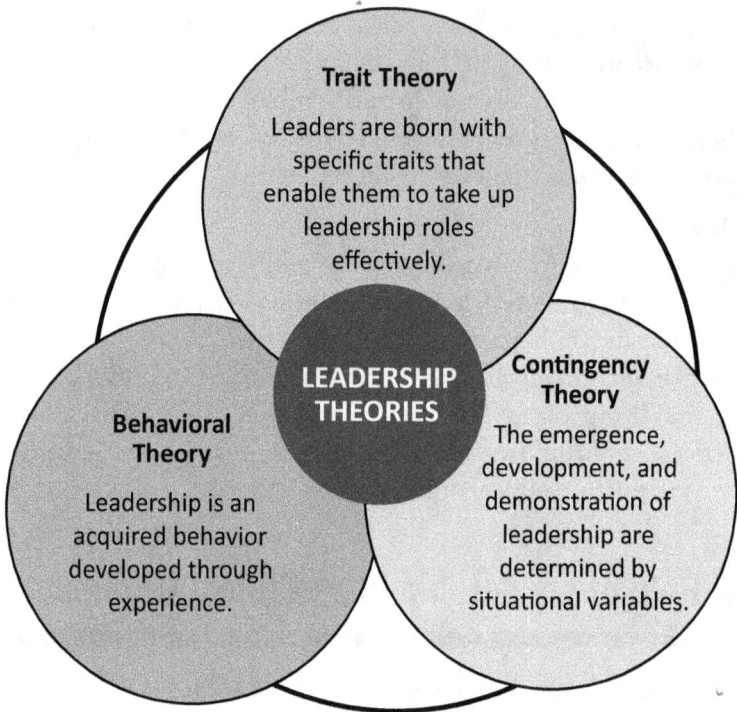

All these theories can explain the role of leaders in building ethical organizations, as discussed below:

Trait theory

According to the trait theory, leaders are born with specific traits that enable them to take up leadership roles effectively. It states that leadership skills emerge from specific traits in an individual. These traits may include empathy, extroversion, reliability, and self-confidence. They also include team-building ability, emotional stability, resilience, and self-efficacy.

The Big Five Traits Theory has been empirically tested to be reliable for predicting leadership behavior (Goldberg, 1990[86];

---

86. Lewis R. Goldberg, "An Alternative 'Description of Personality': The Big-Five Factor Structure," *Journal of Personality and Social Psychology* 59, no. 6 (1990): 1216-1229. https://doi.org/10.1037/0022-3514.59.6.1216

Costa and Robert, 1992[87]). According to this theory, leadership personalities are based on traits like high extraversion, openness to experience, conscientiousness, agreeableness, and low neuroticism. People with these traits demonstrate leadership behavior when placed in a demanding environment.

As per the trait theory, genetic influences and ensuing personality traits like accountability, empathy, compassion, fairness, respect, and being value-driven, influence the quality of decisions taken by the leader. For instance, retail individual investors may trust a family business led by multiple generations based on the belief that personality traits influencing ethics are being transferred from one generation to another.

Behavioral theory

On the other hand, behavioral theory propounds that leadership is an acquired behavior developed through experience. This behavior is marked by activities that show concern for people, for the company, or both.

Following the behavioral theory, the demonstration effect applies. A leader who exhibits resilience while making the right choices and sticks by those choices despite the consequences will inspire trust. Such a leader encourages employees by demonstrating that the company supports them in choosing the right option. This approach is key to motivating employees and building an ethical organization. Similarly, a leader who despises corruption in any form in personal and professional life shall be able to set an example for employees to abstain from being involved in any corruption.

Contingency theory

The contingency theory suggests that the emergence, development, and demonstration of leadership are determined

---

87. Paul T. Costa Jr. and Robert R. McCrae, "Revised NEO Personality Inventory (NEO-PI-R) and NEO Five-Factor Inventory (NEO-FFI) Professional Manual," Odessa, FL: Psychological Assessment Resources, 1992.

by situational variables. In other words, leadership behavior is contingent upon the conditions a person faces. The contingency theory also suggests that only leaders who face critical situations or crises, wherein they are expected to make the right choice against all odds, can truly stand the test of time. These leaders are the ones who can nurture and sustain an ethical organization.

During the COVID-19 pandemic, many business leaders faced the ethical dilemma of whether to retain employees or lay them off. They were forced to make these difficult choices as companies faced financial difficulties. The ones who chose humanity over profit-making in the challenging pandemic could sustain long-term relationships with their employees. Their choice of protecting employees spoke about their grit and ethical qualities amid the crisis.

> Further learning (link also available in Online Resources)
> **"Lecture on Ethics and Leadership"** https://bit.ly/3QfWzF5

Literature also explains leadership from the impact angle. Leaders may be transactional or transformational.[88] While transactional leaders focus on transactions, i.e., interaction yielding results, transformational leaders mentor and spur innovation for the long-term transformation of employees and the organization.

For instance, transactional leaders would only be interested in discussing agenda points related to work-related input and outcomes. In contrast, transformational leaders will ensure that the followers also grow personally while working with them in the organization. Employees must become better at handling their tasks through the leadership.

Let's look at the difference between transactional and transformational leadership, with examples in Table 6.1 below:

---

88. Fred E. Fiedler, *A Theory of Leadership Effectiveness* (New York: McGraw-Hill, 1967).

Table 6.1	Transactional and transformational leadership	
Concept	**Definition**	**Example**
Transactional Leadership	Focuses on transactions, i.e., interactions yielding results	A transactional leader might set specific targets for employees. They provide rewards or consequences based on whether those targets are met.
Transformational Leadership	Mentors and spurs innovation for the long-term transformation of employees and the organization, relying on organizational vision and long-term development	A transformational leader inspires employees to innovate and develop new ways of working. This leads to the long-term growth of individuals and the organization.

(Source: Burns, 1978;[89] Bass, 1985[90])

From an ethical standpoint, transformational leaders are more instrumental in promoting an ethical culture because they do not focus on short-term outcomes; they rely on organizational vision and the long-term development of individual and organizational potential. While such leadership can be truly rewarding in promoting ethics, there are challenges. The following section discusses challenges, opportunities emerging from these challenges, and specific best practices applicable in real-world settings.

---

89. James Burns MacGregor, *Leadership* (New York: Harper & Row, 1978).

90. Bernard M. Bass, *Leadership and Performance Beyond Expectations* (New York: Free Press, 1985).

6.3 Leadership Challenges, Opportunities, and Best Practices

There is a critical need for more leaders to build ethical organizations. To begin with, one takes time to understand ethics and assess and evaluate ethical dilemmas. Such dilemmas often fall into the grey zones where right and wrong choices merge, and more clarity is needed on the right choice. This abstractness and lack of clarity may be uncomfortable for some leaders.

Those able to deal with uncertainty, process diverging interests, vast information, and opposing viewpoints become influential leaders. Those who nurture ethical organizations must also have the courage to confront opinions that favor short-term profitability and immediate outcomes. They have a clear vision to institutionalize ethical decision-making.

Ethical leadership challenges in organizations also present opportunities. Governments support ethical leaders and organizations through policies and regulations that encourage ethical behavior. Another factor favoring ethical leadership is that ethics usually overlap legal implications. Further, stakeholder awareness is rising. All parties from consumers and investors, to employees are demanding greater accountability and ethical conduct from organizations. Social media amplifies this trend by providing a public platform to hold companies accountable and promote fair, positive behavior.

Regarding best practices, organizations with clear standard operating procedures and policies can ensure consistent ethical practices. Clear guidelines help employees, suppliers, and other stakeholders understand the expected behaviors. They enable stakeholders to make the right decisions aligned with the company's values. Effective communication and engagement with stakeholders is also crucial. Leaders can build trust and loyalty by actively involving stakeholders in decision-making and ensuring a diversity of perspectives. However, communication must be continuous and strategic. It should also be tailored to be suitable for the type of stakeholder.

Leaders who encourage adherence to international standards, such as the Global Reporting Initiative (GRI) and the International Integrated Reporting Council (IIRC), enhance credibility and commitment to ethical practices. By embracing such emerging best practices, leaders can create a strong foundation for long-term success. They can pave the path for positive social impact through ethical organizations.

Further learning (link also available in Online Resources)
"The ROI of Ethical Leadership in Business" https://bit.ly/3QgABSe

6.4 Role of Corporate Governance in an Ethical Organization

Governance refers to the role played by the top governing body within the organization. It determines the overall direction and control over the business by operationalizing the vision and mission. Critical decisions concerning the future of the organization are affected by governance.

Governance also plays a role in influencing the ethical culture of an organization, and determining how it pursues ethical goals and objectives. The quality of governance impacts the organization's compliance with legal standards and societal values. It also contributes to fulfilling stakeholder expectations.

The company's board is responsible for drafting and committing to long-term business goals. It must also formulate and implement strategic plans to achieve these goals. It also sets boundaries for achieving goals. For instance, the board of directors must always approve a code of conduct manual.

Let's find out through Table 6.2, how the role of corporate governance is different from that of the management and administration in an organization:

Table 6.2 **Difference in governance, management and administration roles**

Concept	Role
Governance	The board of a company approves the company's goals. It also supervises the ethical standards to be adhered to achieve these goals.
Administration	The administrative staff organizes ethics training programs and reports any deviances so management can take appropriate action.
Management	Management may direct employees to choose sustainable vendors to comply with ethical supply chain practices, even if it involves higher costs.

The administrative staff is also responsible for executing the policies and procedures that the management develops. They ensure that employees comply with the code of ethics and report any deviance. Management, on the other hand, has decision-making authority and power. Policies are made by management based on the direction of the governing body, to be executed by the administrative staff.

Management decisions affect daily activities and the management team is responsible for them during uncertain times. Managers ensure that employee performance and organizational outcomes are achieved through ethical means. They deal with deviations, if any.

There are many corporate governance regulations across the world. Overall, the objectives of all these regulations are similar, i.e., to promote transparency. By ensuring fairness and accountability, they promote ethical values. The following Table 6.3 sheds more light on these objectives:

Table 6.3	**Corporate governance objectives**

Concept	Definition	Example
Transparency	The purpose of transparency is to improve the quality and quantity of disclosures.	The boards are mainly focused on strategic decision-making. They establish codes of conduct and approve mechanisms for dealing with unethical behavior. They facilitate regular and detailed reporting of the company's activities to stakeholders.
Fairness	Refers to equal voice, representation, and opportunity for different stakeholders.	The board ensures all stakeholder interests are considered and balanced in decision-making processes.
Accountability	Responsible for one's actions and plans to promote ethical values within the organization.	The board establishes ethics committees, sets executive compensation policies, and conducts audits of ethical practices to ensure accountability

The Sarbanes Oxley Act is a widely known measure for corporate governance in America.[91] The Act came into existence due to major corporate scandals in companies such as Enron and WorldCom. It was conceptualized to ensure strict monitoring of financial irregularities, frauds, window dressing, or cheating by management and employees.

In the UK, the UK Corporate Governance Code applies.[92] It explains regulatory provisions related to board size and composition, duties of directors, and privileges including remuneration, relations with shareholders etc. Other countries also have similar regulations for corporate governance.

---

91. "Sarbanes-Oxley Act," accessed July 12, 2024, https://www.law.cornell.edu
92. "UK Corporate Governance Code," accessed July 20, 2024, https://www.frc.org.uk

Some international guidelines like the Organization for Economic Cooperation and Development[93] (OECD) and the United Nations Principles of Responsible Investment[94] (UNPRI) also exist. The OECD guidelines help governments to evaluate the legal, institutional, and regulatory framework for corporate governance. On the other hand, the UNPRI guidelines provide a framework to promote financing for sustainability.

6.5 Best Practices of Corporate Governance

The structure and composition of the boards are significant. They must reflect the interests of diverse stakeholders. Boards must be inclusive but they must also reach a consensus to meet stakeholders' needs on one hand and achieve the company's financial and market performance goals on the other. Ensuring this balance can be challenging.

These challenges create room for opportunities for the board, to promote best governance practices for ethical organizations. This is discussed in detail in the following Table 6.4:

Table 6.4   **Corporate governance best practices**

Concept	Definition	Example
Integrating Sustainability and CSR	Boards can ensure an ethical culture by integrating sustainability and CSR into their agendas.	The board discusses and implements policies that help organizations meet regulatory requirements and commit to social and environmental responsibility.

---

93. "OECD," accessed July 12, 2024, https://www.oecd.org
94. "United Nations Principles of Responsible Investment," accessed July 12, 2024, https://www.unpri.org

Concept	Definition	Example
Board Structure and Composition	The collective wisdom of the board determines the effectiveness of corporate governance.	Boards include members with diverse skills and experiences, ensuring adequate representation of various stakeholders' interests.
Independent Directors	Independent directors are those with no financial interests in the organization's objectives. Such directors must be adequately represented on the board to ensure balanced and bias-free decision-making.	The board includes independent directors to provide unbiased and fair strategic guidance.
Regular Meetings and Prepared Agendas	To ensure proper governance, the boards must meet regularly. Adequately prepared agendas must be communicated well in advance to board members.	The board schedules frequent meetings, prepares detailed agendas, and meticulous documentation, with room for dissent.
Specialized Committees	Establishing specialized committees to ensure focused governance	The board forms audit, risk, and ethics committees to handle specific governance areas.
Transparent Communication	Timely and transparent communication of information to board members and stakeholders	The board ensures all decisions, policies, outcomes, and relevant information are communicated to all stakeholders.
Prompt Decision-Making	Making timely decisions to address emerging challenges and opportunities effectively	The board acts quickly to address new issues or opportunities. This ensures the organization can adapt to changes in the competitive environment.

By adhering to these best practices, boards can ensure ethical organizational cultures. This leads to sustainable success in a competitive global environment.

Discussion Questions

1. Explain the role of leadership in an ethical organization from the trait theory perspective.

2. Distinguish between transformational and transactional leadership. Which of these is more critical for an ethical organization?

3. Explain the difference between the role of governance, management, and administration in promoting ethical culture in an organization.

4. Why is diversity and inclusion important in board structures?

5. Discuss the best practices in corporate governance for nurturing ethical organizations.

Chapter Summary

◆ Leadership and corporate governance are essential for building an ethical organization.

◆ Leaders may be born or made. Trait, behavioral as well as contingency theories can be used to explain the role of leaders in ethical organizations.

◆ There is a need for more leaders with ethical values, who demonstrate ethical behaviors under challenging situations.

◆ Corporate governance refers to the role played by the top governing body, i.e., the board of directors in a business organization. Corporate governance aims to achieve the vision and mission of the organization.

◆ Corporate governance promotes ethical cultures by ensuring fairness, accountability, and transparency.

◆ Factors such as the size and structure of the board of directors, the frequency of their meetings, and the meticulousness with which the meetings are conducted determine the efficiency and effectiveness of governance mechanisms.

Quiz

1. **What does Trait Theory suggest about leaders?**

   a. Leaders are made through experience.

   b. Leadership behavior is contingent upon the situation.

   c. Leaders are born with specific traits that enable them to lead effectively.

   d. Leadership is determined by the context in which a leader operates.

2. **According to Behavioral Theory, leadership is:**

   a. Inherent and not changeable

   b. Developed through experience and concern for people or company

   c. Dependent on situational factors

   d. A function of specific traits possessed by individuals

3. **Contingency Theory posits that:**

   a. Leaders are born with traits that make them effective.

   b. Leadership effectiveness depends on the situation and conditions.

   c. Leadership behavior is static and unchanging.

   d. Leaders are made through learned behavior.

4. **Which of the following best describes Transformational Leadership?**

   a. Focuses on transactions and short-term outcomes

   b. Mentors and inspires long-term growth and innovation

   c. Relies solely on adherence to established procedures

   d. Emphasizes immediate results and rewards

5. **Which leadership style is associated with setting specific targets and providing rewards based on those targets?**

   a. Transformational leadership

   b. Transactional leadership

   c. Behavioral leadership

   d. Contingency leadership

6. **Which of the following is a best practice for leaders to promote ethical behavior?**

   a. Establishing unclear ethical guidelines

   b. Communicating transparently and involving stakeholders

   c. Restricting access to information

   d. Avoiding engagement with external stakeholders

7. **Ethical corporate governance primarily involves:**

   a. Executing daily operations and managing employee performance

   b. Setting up and implementing ethical policies and procedures

   c. Conducting internal audits and managing administrative tasks

   d. Ensuring compliance with legal regulations and managing marketing strategies

8. **How does governance differ from administration and management?**

   a. Governance is responsible for day-to-day operational tasks.

   b. Administration executes policies, while governance sets direction.

   c. Management ensures compliance with external regulations.

   d. Administration sets strategic goals for the organization.

9. **Which objective of corporate governance involves increasing the quality and quantity of disclosures?**

   a. Accountability

   b. Fairness

   c. Transparency

   d. Administration

10. **What role do independent directors play in corporate governance?**

    a. They ensure decisions are made without bias and with balanced perspectives.

    b. They are responsible for the day-to-day management of the company.

    c. They handle administrative tasks related to ethics.

    d. They set the company's operational policies.

Answers	1 – c	2 – b	3 – b	4 – b	5 – b
	6 – b	7 – b	8 – b	9 – c	10 – a

This page is intentionally left blank

Chapter 7

Ethics in Marketing and Advertising

KEY LEARNING OBJECTIVES

- Explain the role of ethics in marketing and advertising.
- Discuss case studies and global perspectives on marketing ethics.
- Describe key issues and best practices in this field.
- Analyze challenges and the future of marketing ethics.

This chapter presents an overview of ethics in marketing and advertising. It begins with an explanation of marketing and advertising concepts, followed by the role of ethics in these business functions. The following sections discuss case studies and global perspectives on marketing ethics. Some major ethical concern areas such as labeling, supply chain management, advertising, and social issues, are also discussed in the chapter. It concludes with a discussion of the best practices to implement ethics in marketing and advertising.

7.1 Introduction

Marketing is the creation, communication, and delivery of value to customers. Different stakeholders such as business partners, clients, civil society organizations, and the community are involved in the process of marketing. It may seem that marketing is exclusively about selling the product, however, it begins as soon as the products or services are planned to be created and delivered. It includes market research, internal brainstorming, conceptualization, and design. It also comprises of activities such as distribution, promotion, sales, and the delivery of after-sales services. Thus, advertising falls under marketing.

According to the American Marketing Association, *"Advertising is the placement of announcements and messages in time or space by business firms, nonprofit organizations, government agencies, and individuals who seek to inform and/ or persuade members of a particular target market or audience regarding their products, services, organizations or ideas"*.[95]

The purpose of advertising is to communicate the company's values and brand to potential and existing customers and consumers. It creates awareness and brand equity. It shapes consumers' expectations, perceptions, and loyalty to owning the company's products or services. From an ethical standpoint, advertising is a critical element of marketing. Given their significance, the ethical considerations in marketing and advertising are discussed in this chapter.

7.2 Role of Ethics in Marketing and Advertising

Ethics in marketing and advertising are essential because messages created and conveyed to consumers must be honest, verifiable, and socially responsible. Apart from bringing

---

95. "American Marketing Association," accessed July 12, 2024, https://www.ama.org

commercial success to a business, these messages also impact consumers' consumption patterns and lifestyles.

Businesses are driven by hyper-competition and a mindset to succeed at all costs. This may lure them to indulge in greenwashing or social washing in their marketing and advertising efforts. Greenwashing is when a company proclaims to be "environmentally friendly." It presents its products and services to be good for the environment. However, it does not take any concrete steps toward achieving such outcomes. For instance, a beverage company that causes severe damage to underground water tables but spends considerable money on public relations related to saving water is guilty of greenwashing.

Similarly, social washing is when the company's public relations department exaggerates or fabricates the company's pro-social image while not significantly contributing to society. In the same example, the company may be using high amounts of refined or processed sugar in its products but prints words like "good for you," "low calories," "natural," "healthy," and so on its packaging material; this is indulging in social washing.

Table 7.1	Greenwashing and social washing
Concept	**Examples**
Greenwashing	Green color packaging, nature-inspired logos, misleading eco-labels, "all-natural" claims, "Eco-friendly" buzzwords, fake sustainability certifications, biodegradable claims without proof
Social Washing	Diversity in ads without action, fair trade claims without certification, overstated charity contributions, ethical sourcing false labels, feminism-themed marketing without support, false health benefit claims

(Source: Pope et al., 2016)[96]

---

96. Shawn Pope and Arild Wæraas, "CSR-Washing Is Rare: A Conceptual Framework, Literature Review, and Critique," *Journal of Business Ethics*, no. 137 (2016): 173-193.

Ethical cultures help a firm make decisions that benefit the environment, society, and the firm in the long run. Practices that align with the firm's ethics also promote consumer trust and loyalty, which strongly influence the company's long-term success and brand equity.

Through its investigations over the last few years, Greenpeace has highlighted the role of fast food chains like McDonald's in causing deforestation and fires in Amazon rainforests.[97] Natural forests and habitats are being destroyed to supply these companies. While McDonald's has attempted to address these claims, the problem runs deep. Without ethics integrated into the companies themselves, it is difficult for external stakeholders to enforce ethical practices upon the firms.

> Further learning (link also available in Online Resources)
> **"Every Step Counts to Save the Amazon"** https://bit.ly/4jR8uH3

Ethics also provide a point of reference to the employees. Employees understand the need to ensure communication is consistent with company values and principles, to meet societal expectations, to address customers' needs, and to promote brand equity. The next section discusses some common concerns in marketing and advertising ethics.

7.3 Key Issues and Concerns of Ethics in Marketing and Advertising

Following are some key concerns related to ethics in marketing and advertising practices:

---

97. "Greenpeace," accessed July 23, 2024, https://www.greenpeace.org

Targeting children

One significant concern is the placement and targeting of children in marketing and advertising (Oates et al., 2002[98]; Calvert, 2008[99]). While adults can make their own buying decisions, children are vulnerable and need to be protected. They may be unduly influenced by persuasive marketing strategies and lured to buy products harmful to them.

One example in this regard includes casting children in fizzy drink advertisements. This may end up influencing kids to buy these products. Even if children are not customers but are cast in advertisements, say in the case of detergents, it tends to influence young kids to convince their families to buy these products.

In some countries, this may be legal; in others, very strict regulations target children. Some ban all television advertising aimed at children below 12 years. There are several laws in the United States, from mandatory placement of educational content to restrictions on products where children are the audience.

Social issues

Another contemporary issue is using superficial or opportunistic content related to social issues like LGBTQ+ rights, feminism, or current news events in advertising campaigns. There are pros as well as cons. While this may be a good idea to attract attention, generate a buzz, or ride the social media wave, it may backfire.

For instance, a company that has never advocated for LGTBQ+ rights through its products or campaigns may be guilty of rainbow washing if it mentions its rights only during Pride Month. Superficial attempts are now easier to identify, given the power of social media in the hands of consumers.

---

98. C. Oates, M. Blades, and B. Gunter, "Children's Understanding of Television Advertising: A Qualitative Approach," *Journal of Marketing Communications* 8, no. 2 (2002): 59-71. https://doi.org/10.1080/13527260210122048

99. Sandra L. Calvert, "Children as Consumers: Advertising and Marketing," *The Future of Children* 18, no. 1 (2008): 205-234. https://doi.org/10.1353/foc.0.0001

Misleading labeling

Labeling is also an ethical concern. As the debate on the harmful impacts of toxic chemicals, pollution in the environment, and fast lifestyles on human health intensifies, companies are resorting to marketing strategies aimed at positioning their products and services in the category of healthy and safe offerings. One may find misleading claims such as "now low calorie," "more natural," or "healthier" on food packets, while their sugar or chemical content may not be altered at all.

In one instance, a fast fashion company marketed its recycling initiatives where it had only recycled the cloth tags rather than the clothes. Consumers are becoming aware of and skeptical of such issues. However, we must follow label laws and enforce strict punishments for those violating them.

Celebrity endorsements

Celebrity endorsements also present an ethical dilemma. It is common for sportspersons, artists, and other public figures to be hired to promote products and services. Social media marketing has created a new category of endorsements by influencers. The ethical dilemma relates to the honesty and integrity of celebrities and/or influencers.

While celebrities may motivate people to use certain products, they may not verify the ingredients or use the products themselves. This potentially misleads their followers and fans. Youngsters and children might carry wrong messages home if they idolize these celebrities.

Responsibility in the supply chain

The concerns for ethical marketing are not limited to the company. They extend across the supply chain. While companies may focus on creating ethical products, communicating transparently, embracing social and environmental concerns, and ensuring stakeholder collaboration, it may be challenging to ensure the same across their value chains.

Leading garment manufacturers have been accused of importing from factories in Bangladesh, where laborers work in miserable conditions. The companies responded with ethical sourcing measures to deal with such concerns. Moreover, consumers today are aware and proactive in demanding responsibly sourced products, contributing to an ethical ecosystem.

To promote ethical marketing, marketing managers must ensure that all marketing communications are truthful and socially responsible. The departments may arrange ethical training for employees to uphold the company's values along with stakeholders' concerns and trust. This shall enable them to adopt modern marketing practices while maintaining integrity and long-term customer loyalty.

7.4 Case Studies

Following are some relevant case studies related to ethics in marketing and advertising practices:

Patagonia

Patagonia is a company known for its highly durable outdoor clothing. The company is famously associated with the "Don't buy this jacket" campaign launched during a Black Friday sale. Through this campaign, the company claimed to want to highlight the need for consumers to be conscious about consumption. The campaign was very successful.

However, it was later criticized because it led to an increase in sales rather than a decrease in sales, which was the intended purpose of the campaign. Thus, the campaign backfired in some sense. According to some critics, it is referred to as a case of greenwashing rather than a socially and environmentally responsible initiative.[100]

---

100. "Patagonia Case Study," accessed July 12, 2024, https://www.mckinsey.com

Pepsi

Pepsi is a world-renowned beverage company. The company has established a very strong presence through marketing and advertisement for many years since its inception. It has targeted different age groups, especially the youth, by hiring famous public icons for its advertisements.

Lately, the company has started facing backlash due to the high sugar content in its beverages. Also, it has been guilty of groundwater exploitation and unsustainable farming practices. Taking charge of the current situation and market demands, the company has heavily invested in sustainability initiatives. These initiatives range from supporting farmers and changing its product portfolio, to including low-sugar and healthier alternatives.[101]

McDonald's

McDonald's is a well-known fast-food franchise business. While it is popular among kids due to its positioning and branding activities, it has been involved in many ethical issues. To begin with, it has been held guilty of causing deforestation in Amazon rainforests due to its need for feeding cattle.

Further, many political activists and health experts have written about the harmful effects of consuming its food. McDonald's has tried to address this issue by offering reports about its commitments to environmentally and socially responsible initiatives. It has also made changes in its menus - like the Happy Meal, to offer healthier products to customers.[102]

Ikea

Ikea is known for selling low-cost, contemporary, and modern furniture. The company's unique selling points are its designs, customization facilities, and prices. It manages prices through bulk purchases and transfers furniture assembly to customers.

---

101. Prathamesh Mazumdar, "A Study of Business Process: Case Study Approach to PepsiCo," available at SSRN 2392611 (2014).

102. "McDonald's Case Study," accessed July 12, 2024, https://ivypanda.com

Ikea claims to be people and planet-positive and reports using only sustainable cotton and FSC-certified wood.

However, the Ikea business model encourages people to buy more furniture because it is cheap and not durable. This creates an ironic situation where Ikea claims to be 100% sustainable on the one hand, and on the other, it encourages fast consumption. Thus there is an ethical dilemma facing this business organization.[103]

H&M

H&M is associated with ethical issues related to labor rights and fast fashion. In the case of labor rights concerns, it has been argued that H&M sources garments from factories in Bangladesh. Workers in these factories are said to be employed at cheap rates in hazardous working conditions.

In the latter case of fast-fashion ethical concerns, the company, like other clothing brands, has been accused of promoting fast fashion by launching new designs quickly. This renders the previous designs dated and out of fashion. H&M has tried to address these concerns by launching sustainability initiatives, publishing a sustainability report, and working on a conscious clothing line. However, challenges are complex and continue to be sustained.[104]

Further learning (link also available in Online Resources)
"The Neuroethics of Advertising" https://bit.ly/3X2CQMJ

---

103. "Ikea Case Study," accessed July 12, 2024, https://hbr.org

104. Bin Shen, "Sustainable Fashion Supply Chain: Lessons from H&M," *Sustainability* 6, no. 9 (2014): 6236-6249.

7.5 Best Practices for Ethical Marketing and Advertising

Based on the previous discussion, we may reflect on the best practices for ethical marketing and advertising:

Consistent stance

To begin with, a company must try to maintain a consistent stance and avoid opportunistic behavior. Brands are based on select core values, so communication regarding the brand must be synchronized with these values. This can help the brand to build customer loyalty.

Clear guidelines

Further, clear guidelines explaining the marketing do's and don'ts must be established and communicated to the employees. Such documentation will enable everyone in the organization to understand the core values. Internal communication of these guidelines ensures that everyone adheres to the brand's ethical standards.

Internal communication

Some organizations use a marketing or brand mantra for internal communication and understanding. When Disney started encountering a problem with its marketing channels, it stuck to the mantra of "fun," "family," and "entertainment." These three prerequisites were to be met for any channel, or it would be dropped off the list.

Value creation

Finally, all marketing strategies must not merely aim to sell but to provide better products and create value to improve human lives. By solving genuine problems, companies can build a reputation for trustworthiness with their customers.

7.6 Challenges and the Way Forward

The business environment is challenging. The real world's volatility, uncertainty, complexity, and ambiguity (VUCA) drive business trends.[105] Ethical standards and expectations are also difficult to deal with due to globalization. A firm has to navigate all these challenges through its marketing strategies.

The VUCA world demands resilience and flexibility, and globalization expects firms to have the ability to manage diverse stakeholders' needs. Social media also presents challenges as well as opportunities. It can lend a voice to ethical decisions of a firm, reaching a large number of people in diverse geographical areas in a short period. On the other hand, sometimes, controlling the negative narrative that might start going viral on social media becomes impossible.

The way forward is for firms to have a global mindset while maintaining transparency and a commitment to humanity. Brands must respect cultural differences and ensure inclusive marketing strategies. Transparency will be the future of marketing. Brands can build lasting relationships with their customers by being transparent and socially responsible.

---

105. "VUCA," accessed July 12, 2024, https://hbr.org

Discussion questions

1. Explain the role of ethics in advertising with the help of an example.

2. What is rainbow washing? How can one identify it?

3. What are the ethical concerns of casting children in advertisements?

4. What is the purpose of marketing from an ethical standpoint?

5. Discuss a case study of an organization that violated ethical norms and its repercussions for the firm.

Chapter Summary

◆ Marketing is the process of creating, communicating, and delivering value to customers. Advertising is a very critical part of marketing.

◆ Some common ethical issues are featuring children in advertisements, non-transparent labeling, supply chain impacts, overselling social issues, and misleading celebrity endorsements.

◆ Firms use social, green, and rainbow-washing to market their products or services and, thus, need to evaluate their policies for ethical issues and concerns. Cases in this regard include Patagonia, Ikea, McDonald's, H&M, and Pepsi.

◆ The best practices for ethical marketing include maintaining a consistent stance, establishing clear guidelines and a brand mantra, embracing a global mindset, and directing marketing efforts toward improving human lives.

Quiz

1. **According to the American Marketing Association, advertising is defined as:**
    a. The process of creating products and services
    b. The placement of announcements and messages to inform and persuade target markets
    c. The development of marketing strategies and sales plans
    d. The execution of market research and product testing

2. **What role does ethics play in marketing and advertising?**
    a. Ensures messages are deceptive to gain a competitive advantage
    b. Requires messages to be honest, verifiable, and socially responsible
    c. Focuses solely on maximizing short-term profits
    d. Prioritizes aggressive marketing tactics over customer welfare

3. **What is greenwashing?**
    a. A strategy to genuinely promote environmentally friendly products
    b. Claiming environmental benefits without significant actions to support them
    c. Implementing rigorous environmental standards in product development
    d. Transparently communicating a company's sustainability efforts

4. **Social washing refers to:**

   a. Accurate portrayal of social issues in marketing campaigns

   b. Exaggerating or fabricating a company's pro-social image without accurate contributions

   c. Genuine support for social causes through marketing efforts

   d. Involving social issues only to enhance brand reputation

5. **Which ethical concern involves misleading claims about a product's attributes?**

   a. Targeting children

   b. Misleading labeling

   c. Celebrity endorsements

   d. Social issues

6. **What is a key issue with targeting children in advertisements?**

   a. Children are not influenced by marketing messages.

   b. Children are legally protected from being marketed to.

   c. Children may be unduly influenced by persuasive marketing strategies.

   d. Marketing to children is always ethical and well-regulated.

7. **Which of the following is an example of misleading labeling?**

    a. A company marketing its products as "eco-friendly" while making no fundamental changes

    b. A company advertising a product's actual benefits and features

    c. Clearly stating the product's ingredients and sourcing

    d. Using accurate and truthful claims about a product's health benefits

8. **Ethical concerns with celebrity endorsements include:**

    a. Ensuring celebrities use or believe in the products they endorse

    b. Allowing celebrities to endorse any product without verification

    c. Promoting products without any celebrity involvement

    d. Focusing solely on the celebrity's popularity

9. **What does responsible supply chain management in marketing require?**

    a. Complete transparency and addressing social and environmental concerns

    b. Limiting communication with supply chain partners

    c. Ignoring the social impact of supply chain practices

    d. Focusing only on cost reduction in the supply chain

10. **Pepsi's ethical challenges have included:**
    a. Successful sustainability initiatives and low sugar content
    b. Groundwater exploitation and high sugar content in beverages
    c. Perfect environmental practices and sustainable farming
    d. Completely transparent marketing practices

Answers	1 – b	2 – b	3 – b	4 – b	5 – b
	6 – c	7 – a	8 – a	9 – a	10 – b

This page is intentionally left blank

Chapter 8

Ethics in Human Resource Management

KEY LEARNING OBJECTIVES

- Understand the role of ethics in HRM.
- Analyze ethical dilemmas in HRM and their solutions.
- Describe the best practices in this field.
- Discuss the challenges and the way forward.

This chapter covers ethical issues in Human Resource Management (HRM). The main functions and activities under HRM are explained including hiring, managing, and motivating employees. We will also discuss the difference between strategic and non-strategic HRM. The following sections describe major ethical areas of concern in HRM through the case studies of Walmart, Amazon, Unilever, and Nestlé surrounding these concerns. Best practices and challenges are also discussed in the concluding paragraphs.

8.1 Introduction

In this chapter, we will discuss the role of ethics in HRM. HRM is the function of hiring and motivating people to work toward the organization's goals and objectives.[106] It includes identifying the right talent and getting them on board. It also involves functions such as designing jobs along with compensating and motivating employees.

Traditionally, HRM was associated with a "hiring and firing" role. However, viewing people as a "resource" may not be conducive to motivating employees. Resources diminish when utilized, while people flourish and contribute more to the organization if motivated and managed appropriately. Thus, HRM seems a misnomer and human capital management is a better alternative.

Today, leading organizations consider "HR" a strategic function; because ultimately it is the kind of people one employs, that determines the success or failure of the organization. Strategic HRM aligns HR department goals with the organization's core competency and sustainable advantage.

Further learning (link also available in Online Resources)
"The Strategic Side of HRM" https://bit.ly/3WZDB9k

---

106. Stephen Wood, "Human Resource Management and Performance," *International Journal of Management Reviews* 1, no. 4 (1999): 367-413.

Table 8.1	Difference between HRM and strategic HRM	

Concept	Definition	Example
HRM	The function of hiring and motivating people to work toward the organization's goals and objectives	Traditional HRM roles include hiring, firing, and managing daily personnel activities.
Strategic HRM	Aligns HR department goals with the organization's core competency and sustainable advantage	Leading organizations consider HR a strategic function, determining success or failure based on employee quality.

(Source: Hendry and Pettigrew, 1986)[107]

Ethics in HRM are essential because people must be treated with respect, fairness, and dignity.[108] HRM policies shall determine how people enter and leave the organization, which has far-reaching implications for the company's brand value. It also affects its competitive positioning and financial performance. Thus, prioritizing ethics in HRM is critical for the success of any business organization.

The following section elaborates on the role of ethics in HRM with the help of examples.

8.2 Role of Ethics in Human Resource Management

Natural sciences are different from social sciences. The laws in natural sciences are universally applicable and generalizable.

---

107. Chris Hendry and Andrew Pettigrew, "The Practice of Strategic Human Resource Management," *Personnel Review* 15, no. 5 (1986): 3-8.

108. Michelle R. Greenwood, "Ethics and HRM: A Review and Conceptual Analysis," *Journal of Business Ethics*, no. 36 (2002): 261-278.

However, human behavior may vary in different contexts. Hence, the results of social experiments may not always be generalizable.

Clear and unbiased organizational policies and procedures are essential to deal with uncertainties. Thus, the human resource department's role is crucial in laying the foundation of an ethical organization. This section discusses ethical concerns in different HRM functions and the need for aligned policies for each function.

8.2.1 Recruitment

Recruitment is the process of inviting applications for a vacancy in the organization. After an assessment of the current and future workload, vacancies are identified by the HR department. For these vacancies, applications are invited from prospective candidates through different sources. These sources include online platforms such as LinkedIn, websites, print media, recruitment agencies, and others.

Some common ethical issues regarding recruitment include a lack of transparency in the job advertisement, missing or misleading information, and poor job descriptions. Complete job details are sometimes not provided, or the recruitment process needs to be revised. For instance, an advertisement that neither mentions the package details nor contact details of the HR officials needs more transparency and critical information. While employees want to work with leading employers, the latter also strive for competent employees. Thus, well-designed recruitment strategies enable employers to access good employee candidatures by building the best employer brands.

8.2.2 Selection

Recruitment is followed by selection. It involves reviewing the applications received through recruitment, checking eligibility, and identifying the best candidates for respective vacancies. Selection involves different types of tests. These tests may be related to verbal ability, analytical skills, quantitative aptitude, attitude, skills, knowledge related to job specifications, and interviews.

Some common ethical requirements in the selection process are establishing objective criteria, transparency in the process, reporting, timely communication with employees, and informing the ones not selected with appropriate responses. The best places to work are the ones that take due care of all these concerns. Companies that do not feel the need to respond in time or ghost candidates after interviewing are viewed skeptically in the job market from an ethical point of view.

8.2.3 Compensation

After selection, the organization presents an offer to the candidate. This offer includes working terms and conditions, and the candidate's compensation package. HR managers are responsible for designing objective and fair compensation policies, which leave no room for misinterpretation or bias. Companies that follow transparent compensation policies communicated to employees well on time are considered ethical. Further, companies must ensure equal pay for equal work and no compensation discrimination based on gender, religion, region, economic background, or ethnicity.

8.2.4 Training and development

Training includes organizing workshops and sessions for employees to improve their skills and knowledge. These programs are time-bound and are organized for specific groups of employees on a topic referred by the management, market needs, or as requested by the employees themselves.

Development has a larger ambit. It includes training, mentoring, and support provided to employees at the workplace to help them realize their potential. Ethical issues in training and development concern the allocation of adequate training budgets, and providing an equal chance for employees to upgrade their skills. It also involves ensuring a supportive environment, dealing with toxicity, encouraging employees to upgrade their skills and knowledge proactively, and so on.

8.2.5 Appraisal

Appraisal is the process of evaluating the performance of employees to ascertain performance benefits to be allocated to each employee. It also includes assessing if the employees achieved the objectives set at the beginning of the appraisal period and providing feedback on their performance.

Ethical, modern-day organizations must avoid traditional yearly appraisals, where employees are given feedback once a year in a hierarchical set-up. Agile organizations, allowing employees to experiment, fail fast, and learn from their failures will succeed and lead in the future. Appraisal systems must be designed to be free from bias, encourage experimentation, accept failure, incorporate stakeholders' feedback regularly, and empower the employees rather than doubting them.

8.2.6 People management

Besides hiring-related functions, the HR department also ensures people management by understanding employees' personalities, attitudes, and values. It also assesses job satisfaction, resolves conflict, and motivates employees to achieve organizational outcomes. A key element of policies related to these functions is that the HR department must be strategically empowered to treat employees with equity and dignity.

Organizational behavior researchers have reported that money is not the sole motivator; work culture is crucial in keeping employees engaged and retaining them. Therefore, ethics are a major contributor to the organizational culture. The following Table 8.2 presents popular instances of ethical concerns in different HRM functions:

Table 8.2	Ethical concerns in different HRM functions

HRM Function	Ethical Concerns
Recruitment	Discrimination, nepotism, misleading job descriptions
Selection	Bias, privacy concerns, lack of transparency
Compensation	Pay inequality, unfair bonus distribution, lack of pay transparency
Training and Development	Favoritism, inequitable access, misallocation of resources
Appraisal	Inaccurate assessments, lack of constructive feedback, influence of personal bias
People Management	Harassment, bullying, lack of support for diversity

(Source: Patrick and Mazhar, 2019)[109]

8.3 Case Studies

This section describes case studies of global multinational corporations facing ethical concerns in people management.

8.3.1 Amazon

Amazon is a leading company in the e-commerce industry and has diversified into different sectors. This includes sectors such as technology, supermarket chains, retail, and so on. Despite its global presence, strong competitive position, and large customer base, it has been accused of labor law violations from time to time.

It employs labor-intensive back-end operations in warehouses where employees work long hours on strict delivery schedules. Employees in various locations worldwide have accused the

---

109. Parul Patrick and Shabana Mazhar, "Core Functions of Human Resource Management and Its Effectiveness on Organization: A Study," *International Journal of Social Economics* 9, no. 5 (2019): 257-266.

company of poor working conditions, causing physical and mental strain to workers. The working hours are unusually long, restrooms are unavailable, and spaces are not designed appropriately.

This brought criticism to the company, and they have tried to handle the situation by issuing statements, revisiting policies, and establishing grievance redressal mechanisms. This case provides insight into the need to nurture happy employees for the organization's long-term success.

8.3.2 Walmart

Walmart tops the charts of the global list of Fortune 500 companies.[110] The company is known for its low prices and volume sales. It is also the world's biggest employer. However, like Amazon, it has faced legal hassles related to employee concerns. These concerns include long working hours, poor working conditions, lack of insurance and health coverage, gender and other forms of discrimination.

Given the scale of Walmart, it is challenging to manage the world's largest global workforce. However, irrespective of their size, ethics demand responsibility from businesses. And to treat employees with dignity, respect, and fairness.

8.3.3 Nestlé

Nestlé, a leader in the fast-moving consumer goods industry, is associated with Creating Shared Value (CSV). Within CSV, Nestlé promotes the concurrent pursuit of business and social responsibility by promoting cluster development, i.e., improving employees' lives and organizational outcomes.

Nestlé works closely with its milk farmers and provides them access to basic facilities and an improved quality of life. The ecosystem created for these farmers and their families motivates them to work for the company to achieve its financial goals

---

110. "Fortune 500," https://fortune.com

and obligations. Although a capitalistic pursuit is involved in CSV, it promotes ethical practices related to HRM within the organization.

8.3.4 Unilever

Unilever, headquartered in New Jersey, is known worldwide for its fast-moving consumer goods. The company supports several "people and planet-positive initiatives" through its sustainability plans. It works with many farmers on different continents to produce consumer eatables.[111] It has committed to regenerative agriculture involving practices that sequester carbon in soil and retain its nutrients throughout the year.[112] Crops are grown on the soil on a rotation basis rather than leaving it barren.

The company supports its distant supply chain partners by working on such practices. This isn't directly an employee issue - but an issue concerning people involved in the supply chain. A company that takes care of all partners, communicates that all its stakeholders must embrace an ethical culture.

8.3.5 #MeToo

In 2017, the #MeToo movement became prominent in the media. It was related to the workplace goal of providing all employees with a safe, dignified, equal, and inclusive environment. This is also a core issue in ethical HRM practices. As women started coming out with revelations of sexual harassment faced by them at the workplace, the "#MeToo" moment snowballed into a movement. Social media helped amplify their concerns.

The movement highlighted significant concerns about well-defined workplace harassment laws, transparent procedures, inquiries, and reports. It also highlighted the need to separate power equations from such matters, and for responsible

111. "Unilever," accessed June 20, 2024, https://www.unilever.com
112. "Unilever," accessed June 20, 2024, https://www.unilever.com

leadership behavior. This case demonstrated that organizations will be forced to adopt ethical cultures if employees and stakeholders come together. Thus, for its own benefit, a business organization must pro-actively formulate and implement measures to prevent sexual harassment at work.

8.4 Best Practices for Ethical HRM

The issues discussed in the previous section highlight the initiatives that business organizations must focus on to promote ethical HRM. Some best practices in this context are explained in this section.

Table 8.3   **Best practices for ethical HRM**

Best Practice	Example
Valuing people	Implementing a fair recruitment policy
Supporting employees during crises	Providing financial assistance and support during natural disasters or pandemics
Embedding ethical practices in culture	Regular ethics training programs
Adopting agile and adaptable systems	Implementing flexible work policies

To begin with, valuing people must be the core focus of a business. Businesses must prioritize universal human values and rights over short-term profits. This will be supported by most stakeholders and benefit the company in the long run. This can be executed by ensuring equity, inclusion, and accountability in all the processes related to HRM functions like recruitment, selection, training and development, appraisals, compensation, and so on. Organizations should also provide employees with safe and healthy working spaces and environments.

Second, organizations must follow their values in everyday activities, but their behavior during a crisis is fundamental. Some expectations include financial assistance during employee emergencies, prioritizing the safety of all employees, supporting them during natural disasters and pandemics, and ensuring a better quality of life for all.

Third, HR managers must embed ethical practices in the organizational culture. This can be ensured by hiring the right employees for their culture, organizing regular training programs, clear communication, continuously monitoring HR practices, and dealing with deviances on time.

Fourth, organizations must shift from bureaucratic procedures and hierarchical settings to agile and adaptable systems. Organizations with HRM policies that incorporate uncertainties and modify their systems to match the changed needs will be better equipped to promote ethical cultures. Sometimes, under care ethics, organizations also have to deal with exceptional ethical dilemmas, and decisions must be based on empathy rather than objectivity.

Further learning (link also available in Online Resources)
"Ethics: Yes, Even When Nobody is Watching"
https://bit.ly/4hU28Vp

8.5 Challenges and the Way Forward

The best practices discussed above highlight business initiatives to promote ethical HRM. However, implementing these practices comes with its own set of challenges.

Managing a diverse workforce means dealing with different cultural, religious, regional, social, and individual belief systems. HR policies must be consistent with diverse ethical standards and perspectives, which can be challenging. Global companies like Walmart and Amazon face this challenge by balancing global policies with local customs and laws.

Further, relying on utilitarian ethics may not always be the best way to manage people-oriented organizations. Sometimes, care ethics are needed to demonstrate to the employees that the organization values empathy and compassion. This involves understanding employees' unique situations and making decisions beyond fixed rules and standard procedures to address individual needs. It needs strong leadership and a compassionate work environment.

The integration of Artificial Intelligence (AI) in HRM shall bring its own set of challenges.[113] The advent of AI will affect labor-intensive jobs by replacing certain human tasks with machines. Businesses have already started using technology to manage different aspects of recruitment, selection, training, and development. Employee data are used for several purposes, from finding out why selected candidates did not join to estimating differences in technology acceptance among employees of different generations.

Language models like ChatGPT will also impact the quality and quantity of work and the manpower requirement. As AI advances, companies must establish guidelines for ethical AI use in HRM to prevent potential misuse.

In conclusion, ethics in HRM are critical for a positive and productive work environment. Organizations can promote ethical cultures by understanding the role of ethics in HR and analyzing ethical dilemmas. Other solutions to do this are to implement best practices and address the challenges of diverse perspectives through empathy and the use of AI. These solutions help to motivate employees by prioritizing ethics, ensuring long-term success and sustainability.

---

113. Pawan Budhwar, Ashish Malik, MT Thedushika De Silva, and Praveena Thevisuthan, "Artificial Intelligence–Challenges and Opportunities for International HRM: A Review and Research Agenda," *The International Journal of Human Resource Management* 33, no. 6 (2022): 1065-1097.

Discussion Questions

1. What is the role of business ethics in human resource management?

2. Discuss key ethical concerns in recruiting and selecting employees.

3. How does Nestlé's cluster development approach help the company and its employees?

4. Discuss the difference between agile and traditional organizations from an employee perspective.

5. How will AI change the future of ethical HRM practices? Explain.

Chapter Summary

◆ The purpose of ethics in HRM is to ensure fairness, equity, inclusion, and respect for employees.

◆ Common ethical dilemmas in HRM are related to recruitment, selection, compensation, training, appraisal, and people management.

◆ Best practices include valuing people over profits, supporting employees during crises, embedding ethical practices in organizational culture, and adopting agile, adaptable systems.

◆ Case studies of Amazon, Walmart, Nestlé, Unilever, and the #MeToo movement illustrate various HR ethical issues. They discuss issues such as working conditions, discrimination, and workplace harassment.

◆ Challenges include managing global perspectives, incorporating empathy in decision-making, and integrating AI ethically. As AI advances, companies must establish guidelines for ethical AI use in HRM to prevent potential misuse by organizations and employees.

Quiz

1. **What is the primary function of Human Resource Management (HRM)?**
   a. Managing organizational finances
   b. Hiring and motivating people to work toward the organization's goals
   c. Creating marketing strategies
   d. Developing technology solutions

2. **What distinguishes strategic HRM from traditional HRM?**
   a. Strategic HRM focuses on administrative tasks, while traditional HRM is more strategic.
   b. Strategic HRM aligns HR goals with the organization's core competencies, while traditional HRM focuses on basic personnel management.
   c. Strategic HRM deals only with hiring, while traditional HRM includes employee motivation.
   d. There is no distinction between strategic HRM and traditional HRM.

3. **Why is ethics important in HRM?**
   a. It helps in reducing employee turnover.
   b. It ensures employees are treated with respect, fairness, and dignity.
   c. It improves financial performance.
   d. It increases the organization's market share.

4. **Which of the following is an example of a traditional HRM function?**

    a. Aligning HR goals with the organization's strategy

    b. Developing employee training programs

    c. Conducting job recruitment and managing daily personnel activities

    d. Designing compensation packages

5. **What is a common ethical issue in the recruitment process?**

    a. Lack of transparency in job advertisements

    b. Providing excessive compensation

    c. Overly detailed job descriptions

    d. Immediate hiring decisions

6. **What does the selection process in HRM involve?**

    a. Designing employee compensation packages

    b. Reviewing applications and identifying the best candidates

    c. Organizing training sessions

    d. Conducting performance appraisals

7. **Which of the following is an ethical concern in the selection process?**

    a. Establishing objective criteria

    b. Providing detailed job descriptions

    c. Implementing high compensation packages

    d. Offering unlimited training opportunities

8. **What is a key ethical consideration in compensation management?**

    a. Ensuring equal pay for equal work

    b. Providing excessive bonuses

    c. Offering flexible work hours

    d. Creating ambiguous compensation packages

9. **What is an example of an ethical issue in training and development?**

    a. Allocating adequate training budgets

    b. Providing exclusive training opportunities

    c. Ignoring employee feedback

    d. Offering limited development programs

10. **What is the purpose of performance appraisal in HRM?**

    a. To design employee training programs

    b. To evaluate employee performance and allocate performance benefits

    c. To recruit new employees

    d. To manage employee conflicts

Answers	1 – b	2 – b	3 – b	4 – c	5 – a
	6 – b	7 – a	8 – a	9 – c	10 – b

This page is intentionally left blank

Chapter **9**

Ethics in Finance

KEY LEARNING OBJECTIVES

- Understand the role of ethics in financial management.
- Analyze case studies highlighting ethical issues in financial management.
- Identify best practices for maintaining ethical standards in financial management.
- Describe the challenges for maintaining ethics in financial management.

This chapter covers ethics in procuring, utilizing, and managing finance in a business organization. The first section discusses key ethical concerns related to finance sourcing, capital budgeting, financial reporting, technology, and innovative financing mechanisms. Then, case studies of Enron,[114] WorldCom,[115] Lehman Brothers,[116] American International Group (AIG),[117]

---

114. Yuhao Li, "The Case Analysis of the Scandal of Enron," *International Journal of Business and Management* 5, no. 10 (2010): 37.

115. "WorldCom Case Study," accessed July 12, 2024, https://www.mbaknol.com

116. Rosalind Wiggins, Thomas Piontek, and Andrew Metrick, "The Lehman Brothers Bankruptcy A: Overview," *Yale Program on Financial Stability Case Study* (2014).

117. "AIG Case Study," accessed July 12, 2024, https://insight.kellogg.northwestern.edu

and Tyco International[118] illustrate these ethical concerns. The following sections discuss the best practices in ethical financial management and the associated challenges emerging from the discussion.

9.1 Introduction

Profit-making is neither wrong nor unethical - it is the primary purpose of a business organization. A business organization buys and sells goods and services and creates value from transactions. To keep going and execute various functions, an organization needs funds. The role of business managers is to procure and manage funds in a way that makes the organization self-sustainable. This role is known as financial management.

It includes sourcing, budgeting, utilizing, and evaluating the return of financial resources. In each of these aspects, ethics exist. Thus, profit-making is not unethical, but making a profit ethically is essential. In other words, it is not about the quantum of return but how the return was created.

Ethical financial management must drive the organization toward its goal. This chapter highlights the role of ethics in different aspects of financial management, key concerns and issues, case studies illustrating such issues, best practices, and challenges.

9.2 Role of Ethics in Financial Management

This section discusses some critical decisions in financial management where ethics are essential.

Sourcing finance

To begin with, sourcing finance is the role of a financial manager. There are two primary sources of finance which are

---

118. Lori M. Thanos, "Tyco International Ltd. Case Study: The Implications of Unethical Behavior," *Academic Leadership Journal in Student Research* 3, no. 1 (2015): 7.

debt and equity. Debt includes raising funds from banks, financial institutions, or other lenders at an interest rate. Equity provides ownership to the investor.

In a company's case, equity shareholders are the company's owners. Whether raising debt or equity, the financial manager must abide by the company's ethical code of conduct. This includes raising money from legitimate and legal sources, being honest and transparent to the lenders and the shareholders, and avoiding unreasonable and risky leverage.

Apart from the legal mandates, the owner must also avoid ethical conflicts based on personal experiences and market conditions. For instance, raising money without proper documentation is a legal issue even if the banks' employees offer to compromise with procedures when sanctioning a loan. Moving beyond a legally mandated leverage ratio and risking the owner's capital in adverse anticipated market conditions is also a major ethical issue.

Capital budgeting

The second aspect is capital budgeting, i.e., allocating funds to long-term projects. Popular methods for project evaluation and allocation are net present value, internal rate of return, payback period method, etc. In these methods, the net financial gain to the organization is the criterion for selecting or rejecting projects.

However, in some instances, the project's purpose may be more significant than the short-term financial gain from the project. Such projects may include training and development initiatives, and Research and Development (R&D) investment. They may also include corporate social responsibility commitments. Even if such projects do not meet the short-term return criteria, the organization must invest in these projects from an ethical perspective.

Sometimes, escalation of commitment can also raise an ethical concern. A project that was supposed to be profitable, according to management judgment, may turn out to be a wrong choice.

In other cases, one may continue investing in it due to prior commitment, even after knowing that it is futile to do so!

Financial reporting

Ethics also matter when preparing the financial results of the organization. The commonly accepted financial statements include the profit and loss statements and balance sheets. These statements are prepared following state and federal regulations and organizational practices. Any change in the standards or practices used for preparing the accounts shall be reflected in the financial performance.

An unethical firm and its managers may use window dressing to inflate their accounts or create fictitious assets to show a better performance. Thus, despite the regulations, ethics play a role in reporting financial performance. These reports are to be audited by accountants, and their ethics matter, too.

Technology impact

With the advent of technology, transparency can be improved. Blockchains, for instance, are famous for tracing financial transactions with transparency and accountability. Similarly, digital payments improve an organization's ability to fight corruption. However, technology has challenges, including change management and users' acceptance of the technology.

Emerging financing models

Apart from technology, other business models and sources of finance have also emerged. While not entirely new, tools like crowd-funding and peer-to-peer lending have gained traction in the past few years. Microfinancing and green bonds have also seen considerable growth in recent years as instruments for sustainable development.

Crowd-funding involves raising voluntary contributions from people. It is usually done through the Internet. Peer-to-peer lending enables one to raise money from individuals or organizations directly rather than from intermediary financial institutions. Micro-financing is committed to providing small loans to entrepreneurs, mainly in rural areas, whose applications would usually be rejected by banks or financial institutions for a lack of individual collateral or guarantee. Green bonds are used to finance projects which are suitable for the environment.

In each of these innovative financing mechanisms, ethics prevail. These innovations enable those, with limited access to traditional sources, to raise money and contribute to the economy. They democratize funding opportunities and promote financial inclusion. Micro-finance can also be viewed as a mechanism for poverty alleviation and economic development. Further, green finance is an emerging area that seeks to promote environmental protection and conservation.

Table 9.1	Ethical considerations in financial management
Aspect	**Description**
Sourcing Finance	Financial managers must ethically raise funds through debt or equity, ensuring transparency and legality.
Capital Budgeting	Ethical considerations include investing in projects with long-term benefits (e.g., CSR, R&D) despite short-term metrics
Financial Reporting	Preparation of accurate financial statements in compliance with regulations to prevent unethical practices like window dressing
Technology Impact	Technologies like blockchain and digital payments check corruption, though challenges like change management persist.
Emerging Financing Models	Ethical finance models such as crowdfunding, peer-to-peer lending, microfinance, and green bonds promote financial inclusion and environmental sustainability.

9.3 Case Studies

This section describes cases of companies accused of unethical financial management. The issues mentioned in the preceding section are illustrated through these cases.

Enron

Enron, a company based in Texas, was one of the prominent multinational companies in energy, communication, paper, pulp, and natural gas. Enron's story is quite popular due to unethical financial management. When this fraud came to light, it led to enacting the Sarbanes Oxley Act of 2002.[119]

Enron was guilty of using mark-to-market accounting and special purpose entities. Mark-to-market accounting practices led the company to book profit on striking a deal, irrespective of whether the deal was realized later. Special purpose entities were used by the company to write off liabilities.

Such window dressing and unethical practices helped Enron show inflated figures on its balance sheet.[120] They were also known to manipulate share prices. The management resorted to insider trading and failed to meet minimum corporate governance obligations. Its unethical financial management practices eventually came to light, resulting in Enron's bankruptcy, losses in the share market, government vigilance, and employee unrest. The Sarbanes Oxley Act was created to avoid such cases in the future.

> Further learning (link also available in Online Resources)
> **"The Rise and Fall of Enron"** https://bit.ly/3X09aQq

---

119. Stephen Wagner and Lee Dittmar, "The unexpected benefits of Sarbanes-Oxley," *Harvard Business Review* 84, no. 4 (2006): 133.

120. Dennis Tourish and Naheed Vatcha, "Charismatic leadership and corporate cultism at Enron: The elimination of dissent, the promotion of conformity and organizational collapse," *Leadership* 1, no. 4 (2005): 455-480.

WorldCom

During that time, WorldCom's financial scandal also came to light. WorldCom was one of the biggest telecommunication companies. It was involved in unethical financial management by inflating its financial statements.[121] The management was guilty of manipulating the company's earnings by showing operating expenses as capital expenditures.

They indulged in insider trading by selling their stock before the news of financial irregularities was revealed in the market. The revelation led to the stock market crash - thousands of investors lost money, and employees lost jobs. WorldCom's auditor, Arthur Anderson, who was also the auditor of Enron, failed to perform its role. Following the bankruptcy of both companies, Arthur Anderson lost business and was dissolved.[122]

American International Group (AIG)

American International Group (AIG) is a multinational company based in the USA that deals in finance and insurance. During the global financial crisis in 2008, AIG underwent a significant financial crisis. The company recklessly sold credit default work, a type of insurance, without engaging in any risk measurement management strategy.[123]

The company eventually fell into a financial trap, and the government had to bail it out to avoid economic ripple effects. After several lawsuits, restructuring, and government bail-out, the company eventually managed to come back and continue to exist. However, the crisis is a stark reminder of financial mismanagement and its repercussions.

---

121. "Report of Investigation by The Special Investigative Committee," accessed July 21, 2024, https://www.sec.gov

122. "Report of Investigation by The Special Investigative Committee," accessed July 21, 2024, https://www.sec.gov

123. "AIG," accessed July 20, 2024, https://insight.kellogg.northwestern.edu

Further learning (link also available in Online Resources)
"Warren Buffet Explains the 2008 Financial Crisis"
https://bit.ly/4hCn6bs

Lehman Brothers

The case of Lehman Brothers is significant in the evolution of corporate governance in the USA. As one of the biggest investment banks, Lehman Brothers faced severe financial troubles. Eventually, it succumbed to bankruptcy in 2008.[124] The financial turmoil was majorly caused by reckless lending of subprime loans by the firm. It was also known to acquire high leverage and resort to faulty practices for window dressing financial statements.

When the housing sector crashed, Lehman Brothers could not bear the load and declared bankruptcy despite trying its best. The downfall reignited discussions on corporate governance as the bank impacted the mass public, business organizations, and the economy.

Tyco International

Tyco International was incorporated in Ireland and headquartered in the USA. The company was engaged in the business of security systems and electronics. Its top executives were guilty of drawing massive amounts of money from it through unauthorized bonuses and utilizing it on personal luxuries. They were also involved in the manipulation of stock prices.[125] The company's financial situation worsened so much that its top executives were charged with criminal offenses.

---

124. "Lehmann Brothers 1850-2008," accessed June 20, 2024, https://www.library.hbs.edu

125. "Tyco International: Leadership Crisis," accessed June 25, 2024, https://harbert.auburn.edu

9.4 Best Practices and Challenges

Drawing from the above-mentioned concerns and cases, we may conclude a few best practices for ethical financial management. These practices are discussed in this section.

9.4.1 Best practices

Long-term sustainability

Financial statements are usually prepared for a short period, i.e., a financial or calendar year. However, finances should be managed to keep the organization's long-term sustainability in mind. This will enable the managers to maximize stakeholders' interests and align with ethics.

Transparency and disclosures

Transparency must be maintained, and disclosures regarding any changes in financial structure, capital budgeting decisions, or leverage must be communicated to lenders, investors, employees, etc.

Balanced leverage

Leverage i.e. debt in the firm's capital structure is a double-edged sword. It can help the firm make better returns if the market is doing well. However, it can backfire during downturns in the economy, as the firm may not be able to fulfill even its minimum financial obligations.

Legal and legitimate finance sources

The sources of finance must be legal and legitimate, avoiding any dubious or unethical practices.

Technology usage

Finally, technology usage may be encouraged to improve accountability and maintain a digital record of transactions.

9.4.2 Challenges

Greed

The major challenge in following these practices is greed. A person overpowered by greed can compromise with ethics and shall not be motivated by moral or ethical motives to choose the right way to make money.

Consumerist temptation

Consumerist lifestyles depicted on social media also increase the temptation to take shortcuts rather than invest time and energy in sustaining a healthy, long-term business.

Motivation for ethics

Despite the legal mandate, ethical codes of conduct, and organizational guidelines, there is no stopping one from indulging in fraud if one is not motivated by moral or ethical motives.

Cultural and organizational barriers

Promoting ethics in organizational culture requires setting examples, rewarding ethical behavior, and dealing strictly with deviations.

Resistance to change

The usage of technology comes with challenges such as change management and users' acceptance of the technology.

Discussion Questions

1. What is the role of ethics in capital budgeting decisions?

2. What lessons in ethical financial management can be drawn from Enron and WorldCom?

3. What was Arthur Anderson's role in the Enron and WorldCom case?

4. Explain the best practices in ethical financial management.

5. Discuss the ethical implications of high financial leverage in a firm.

Chapter Summary

◆ Ethical decisions in financial management are related to sourcing funds transparently and legally. It also refers to allocating funds responsibly, reporting accurately, and integrating technology to improve transparency and accountability.

◆ Companies such as Enron, WorldCom, Lehman Brothers, AIG, and Tyco International resorted to unethical practices, such as financial statement manipulation, and insider trading. They were also associated with excessive risk-taking, poor disclosures, and misappropriation of company funds, which led to their downfall.

◆ Best practices for ethical financial management include managing funds with a long-term sustainability perspective, transparency, and timeliness in financial disclosures. Managing leverage, regular and interim financial reporting, and clear communication with stakeholders are also some popular best practices for ethical financial management.

◆ Maintaining ethics in financial management includes challenges such as greed, the temptation to take shortcuts, and social media influence to indulge in unethical practices for a lavish lifestyle.

Quiz

1. **What is the fundamental principle of ethical financial management?**
   a. Maximizing shareholder profit at all costs
   b. Transparency and accountability in financial reporting
   c. Avoiding all forms of debt
   d. Investing only in high-risk ventures

2. **Which case study is an example of unethical financial practices?**
   a. Apple
   b. Google
   c. Enron
   d. Microsoft

3. **How did Enron's unethical practices come to light?**
   a. Through a successful financial audit
   b. By voluntary disclosure from the company
   c. Through investigative journalism and whistleblowing
   d. By winning an ethical business award

4. **What is the key aspect of ethical financial reporting?**
   a. Using complex accounting methods
   b. Providing clear, accurate, and honest financial information
   c. Prioritizing investor interests over ethical considerations
   d. Keeping financial details confidential

5. **What is the impact of ethical leadership on financial management?**

   a. It can lead to higher levels of trust and better financial performance.

   b. It has no significant impact on financial outcomes.

   c. It increases the complexity of financial reporting.

   d. It reduces the need for financial audits.

6. **Which financial practice involves evaluating the feasibility and profitability of long-term investments?**

   a. Budgeting

   b. Capital budgeting

   c. Short-term financing

   d. Tax planning

7. **What is the role of corporate governance in financial management?**

   a. To centralize financial decision-making

   b. To ensure ethical practices and accountability within an organization

   c. To maximize short-term profits

   d. To reduce transparency

8. **Which company faced scrutiny for unethical financial practices involving stock options?**

   a. AIG

   b. Tyco International

   c. Enron

   d. Lehman Brothers

9. **How can technology impact ethical financial management?**
   a. By reducing the accuracy of financial data
   b. By enhancing transparency and efficiency in financial processes
   c. By complicating financial reporting
   d. By eliminating the need for ethical considerations

10. **What was a significant issue in the Lehman Brothers scandal?**
    a. Misleading investors about the company's financial health
    b. Excessive charitable donations
    c. Transparent financial practices
    d. Conservative investment strategies

Answers	1 – b	2 – c	3 – c	4 – b	5 – a
	6 – b	7 – b	8 – b	9 – b	10 – a

This page is intentionally left blank

Chapter **10**

Emerging Trends, Challenges and Directions

KEY LEARNING OBJECTIVES

- Appreciate the emerging trends in the field of business ethics.
- Describe the challenges anticipated due to the new trends.
- Explain strategies and future direction to deal with the challenges.
- Learn about an integrated framework for future business organizations to institutionalize ethics.

This chapter provides insight into trends, challenges, and strategies for business organizations to promote and integrate ethics. It introduces the emerging trends in ethics for businesses operating in a volatile, uncertain, complex, and ambiguous (VUCA) world amid the increasing rate of globalization.[126] Overall, the chapter provides an overview of future developments in business ethics. It also proposes a

---

126. "VUCA," accessed July 12, 2024, https://hbr.org

framework to institutionalize ethics in business from a futuristic perspective.

10.1 Introduction

Business organizations must adapt to the changing climate, or else they shall be out of competition. For instance, Nokia lost its market to Android phones because of its inability to shift to new technology.[127] Similarly, Blockbuster's lack of adaptability to the rental business led to it being overpowered by Netflix's business model.[128]

Today, technology gets outdated and upgraded in a few months. The rate of change in the business environment is multiplying. Competition is fierce, and globalization gives customers access to a broad market. Customer expectations are also uncertain and complex to comprehend. While market research and data to understand customers' expectations are available, it is difficult to predict human behavior completely. The relationships, i.e., cause and effect between business offerings and sales, are also non-linear and challenging to analyze.

In the wake of all these challenges, the global imperative towards sustainable development and integrating social and environmental concerns, organizations must also be prepared to promote policies, practices, and culture to incorporate ethics in decision-making. In the upcoming section, let's explore emerging trends in business ethics which is a crucial step in this direction.

---

127. Juha-Antti Lamberg, Sandra Lubinaitė, Jari Ojala, and Henrikki Tikkanen, "The Curse of Agility: The Nokia Corporation and the Loss of Market Dominance in Mobile Phones, 2003–2013," *Business History* 63, no. 4 (2019): 574-605. https://doi.org/10.1080/00076791.2019.1593964

128. "Blockbuster Case Study," accessed July 12, 2024, https://medium.com

10.2 Emerging Trends in Business Ethics

This section discusses the key trends in business ethics that organizations need to stay informed about:

Figure 10.1 **Emerging trends in business ethics**

1. **CSR**

    While Corporate Social Responsibility (CSR) is an old concept, it has gained momentum recently. Companies are increasingly focusing on giving back to the community through corporate CSR. Businesses have also started reporting their CSR projects and initiatives as part of their annual or standalone CSR reports. Some companies also invest in impact assessments, which help them measure their projects' positive influence on society and the environment. CSR projects are undertaken in areas such as education, health, environmental sustainability, poverty eradication, gender equality, and empowerment.

2. Sustainability

As discussed in the previous chapters, businesses are embracing sustainability. Some trends include offering sustainable products and services, investing in green technologies, and training and capacity building of employees to promote sustainability. Life cycle assessment of products, including Environmental, Social, and Governance (ESG) criteria in supplier selection, collecting and reporting sustainability performance data, and integrating it into the organization's critical decisions are other examples of popular sustainability trends.

3. Digital ethics

With the advent of Industry 4.0, companies are paying attention to digital ethics. Digital ethics is the branch of ethics that governs online interactions and relationships between a company and its stakeholders. It includes the time and cost allocated to such interactions, the response rate, how queries and complaints are handled by employees, data privacy and security, usage of data for predicting human behavior, informed consent, and so on.

4. Corporate governance

Corporate governance in the contemporary environment seeks to maximize the interests of different stakeholders. Fairness, accuracy, and transparency are the pillars of corporate accountability and functioning. Regulations across the world now ensure that firms are responsible for their actions. These include voluntary as well as mandatory regulations revised from time to time to align with the changing needs of the environment.

5. Diversity, equity, and inclusion

Another trend is the focus on Diversity, Equity, and Inclusion (DEI) initiatives. Diversity aims to promote hiring people from different economic, social, religious, regional, ethnic, cultural, and political backgrounds. Equity refers to the equitable treatment of all employees, acknowledging their differences. Inclusion is paying attention to diverse voices and taking these voices, including dissent, into consideration while making decisions.

6. **Artificial intelligence**
   The next trend is related to Artificial Intelligence (AI). With the usage of artificial intelligence, AI ethics have become significant. For instance, ethics may be about integrating ChatGPT into organizational content creation policy, utilizing chatbots for handling customer queries, using software to shortlist interview resumes, replacing trainers with self-paced applications, etc. In all these activities, the absence of a human interface raises ethical issues like reducing the number of jobs, data privacy concerns, and risky machine behavior.

Further learning (link also available in Online Resources)
"AI Is Dangerous, but Not for the Reasons You Think"
https://bit.ly/40UWbkh

7. **Stakeholder engagement**
   As sustainability is gaining ground, companies have started identifying material issues, i.e., the most profound impacts - positive or negative, of their activities. These material issues are identified through a stakeholder consultation process. Hence, there is a growing trend to engage with stakeholders on a regular and timely basis. Stakeholders' interests are sought and policies are designed to fulfill these interests. From an ethical perspective, stakeholder engagement leads to stakeholder wealth maximization.

8. **Supply chain management**
   Ethics are not limited to the organization but extend to the supply chain. Large multinational corporations are also following the trend of verifying social and environmental impacts of their supply chain partners. For instance, Ikea

uses only certified wood and cotton in making furniture, claiming that it tries to minimize the impact of its supply chain activities on the environment.[129]

9. **Whistleblowing**

   Whistleblowing is a phenomenon where employees (past or present) with access to news of misconduct or fraud within an organization, alert and warn the stakeholders about such wrongdoings. Whistleblower laws are becoming stringent and regulators are taking steps to protect whistleblowers. From a utilitarian and duty perspective, whistle-blowing is ethical if we consider the maximum interest of the stakeholders of society, and our duty as members rather than only as employees.

10. **Global business ethics**

   Finally, as globalization increases, people from diverse countries and cultural backgrounds work together. What may be ethical for a person in one part of the world may not be ethical from another's perspective. For instance, traditions related to attire or casual references in language may be very different for two employees. Apart from these hygiene factors, job-related factors such as autonomy in making decisions, flexibility in working, and power distance between managers and workers shall also vary across cultures and subcultures. Ethical policies must converge to promote respect for diversity while maintaining efficiency and productivity.

---

129. "Ikea," accessed July 20, 2024, https://ikea.com

10.3 Challenges in Business Ethics

This section discusses the present and future challenges associated with business ethics.

1. **Globalization**

   Although globalization has already shaped business operations worldwide, finding a consensus that meets diverse needs of the workforce can be challenging. For instance, as countries open boundaries to promote international trade and business operations, the influx of labor might create trouble for the local population. The solution will be to move towards universal global ethics.

2. **Social sustainability**

   In their annual and sustainability reports, companies disclose social and environmental impacts and economic performance. Given the complexity of social systems, it may be difficult for companies to identify and prioritize social issues. It may also be challenging to finalize the relevant geographical region that needs development.

   Globally, financial aid tends to focus on specific regions, and some areas are always low on priority due to topographical constraints, financial issues, or personal biases despite needing support for development. Further, measuring the impact of social projects is also complex.

3. **Environmental protection**

   The next challenge pertains to environmental protection. Usual ways of engaging in environmental sustainability range from simple activities like plantations to significant operational changes like investing in a water recycling plant.

   Significant efforts like the latter, which are influential in creating an impact, always come at a cost to the business, and the profits are affected in the short term. Companies may still not accept shifting from a short-term logic to a long-term, more significant perspective.

4. **Technology integration**

   While technology creates benefits like transparency, accountability, and diversity, it also has cons. Technology integration requires capacity building of employees. It must also be accepted by employees, suppliers, customers, and other stakeholders, and change management can be challenging. For instance, employees may not use the new software that records all transactions online and removes organizational corruption due to resistance to change.

5. **Data privacy**

   The most critical challenge with technology advancement is data privacy and security. Businesses have access to personal information and can use it to their advantage. As a company, the onus is on the governors and management to promote a culture that respects its stakeholders' informed consent and privacy. Balancing profit-making, fighting competitors, and protecting stakeholders simultaneously can be challenging.

6. **Competition**

   No matter what the competitors resort to, an organization must abide by its ethical code of conduct. As competition intensifies, organizations may be tempted to poach employees. While organizations must get the best people to work for them; they must do so ethically. The challenge is to balance these two aspects.

   Similarly, the competitor may engage in unethical supply chains, over-leveraging/ excessive borrowing, or marketing gimmicks. Even at the cost of profit-making, the organization must avoid such unethical practices.

10.4 Strategies for the Future of Business Ethics

This section provides an overview of strategies for building ethical organizations of the future. As organizations become global and diverse, a need for universal ethics shall emerge. However, universal ethics do not imply uniform ethics. One approach may not suit all. A universal approach shall enable every person to embrace their values and yet comply with the non-negotiable ideals followed by the organization.

For instance, an organization may allow its employees to take advantage of any two leaves on their respective festivals rather than making two predetermined leaves mandatory. Therefore, a balanced approach that does not accept any violation of human rights shall define the organizations of the future.

Below are key strategies to shape the future of business ethics:

Documenting expectations

The first strategy for the future of business ethics is documenting expectations to the extent possible, leaving little room for politics and biased interpretations. Conflicts are less likely to occur if the organization communicates the do's and don'ts to the employees. Training and development shall also be helpful in this regard.

Ethical leadership

Second, the culture will be ethical when the management demonstrates ethics and sets an example. The leaders lead when it comes to following the code of ethics. Future organizations may not have powerful hierarchies and boundaries. Hence, the leader-follower bond shall become even more significant.

Leveraging technology

Third, technology can be leveraged to hold people accountable. Recording all transactions, abiding by digital ethics, and formulating policies for AI integration and usage are some of the focal areas where organizations must be prepared to avoid any ethical conflicts.

Timely evaluation

Fourth, timely evaluation and seeking stakeholder feedback can also be strategically beneficial. Audits by ethics committees formed by internal members, or hiring a third-party professional auditor or a social worker, can help get an on-ground perspective of the ethical environment.

Empowering stakeholders

Fifth, empowering stakeholders can help an organization keep a check on its decisions. An organization that provides room for its stakeholders to engage and participate in organizational plans has a better chance of implementing ethical codes of conduct, as diverse organizations try to promote diverse interests.

Core ethical values

Finally, the organization must follow ethics as part of its core values, and not only to comply with regulatory requirements or mandates. Irrespective of the competitor's unethical practices, such an organization will make the right choices. The capitalistic approach of deriving immediate benefits from following ethics does not work; organizations that stick to their values in the long term are eventually the ones that become successful and are respected in the marketplace.

Based on these strategies, a framework is proposed for institutionalizing business ethics in the below Figure 10.2.

Figure 10.2 Framework for ethical organizations

Top Management	• **Ethical Leadership** • **Document Expectations**
Middle Management	• **Training and Development** • **Timely Evaluation and Audits**
Lower level Management	• **Stakeholder Engagement and Empowerment** • **Leverage Technology**

Further learning (link also available in Online Resources)
"How Ethics Will Change the Future of Technology?"
https://bit.ly/3EBPtYS

Discussion Questions

1. How will artificial intelligence affect business ethics? Discuss.

2. Why is diversity important in an organization? How is it different from inclusion?

3. How can empowering stakeholders help in building an ethical organization?

4. What is an ethics audit? Explain.

5. Explain the strategic framework for institutionalizing business ethics.

Chapter Summary

◆ The emerging trends in business ethics include an increased focus on CSR, sustainability, digital ethics, and AI integration. Recent business ethics trends also include corporate governance, diversity and inclusion, stakeholder engagement, supply chain ethics, whistleblowing, and global business ethics.

◆ The challenges associated with these trends are globalization impacts, identifying social sustainability priorities, and managing environmental protection efforts. Other challenges are integrating technology ethically, safeguarding data privacy, and maintaining ethical standards amid competition.

◆ The proposed strategies include documenting ethical expectations, leveraging technology, empowering stakeholders, embedding core values, and continuous evaluation.

Quiz

---

1. **Which of the following is a recent trend in business ethics related to technology?**

   a. Digital ethics

   b. Diversity and inclusion

   c. Corporate governance

   d. Whistleblowing

2. **What is the primary focus of Corporate Social Responsibility (CSR) in modern businesses?**

   a. Reducing operational costs

   b. Investing in new technologies

   c. Giving back to the community

   d. Enhancing employee productivity

3. **Which trend involves businesses adopting practices to protect the environment?**

   a. Stakeholder engagement

   b. Sustainability

   c. Artificial intelligence

   d. Global business ethics

4. **In the context of business ethics, what does AI ethics primarily address?**

   a. Employee training programs

   b. Data privacy concerns

   c. Integration of AI in business operations

   d. Corporate governance practices

5. **What is a significant focus of corporate governance in modern businesses?**

    a. Increasing profitability

    b. Ensuring fair, accountable, and transparent business operations

    c. Expanding market reach

    d. Reducing employee turnover

6. **Which of the following trends emphasizes engaging with various stakeholders to design policies?**

    a. Whistleblowing

    b. Corporate governance

    c. Stakeholder engagement

    d. Digital ethics

7. **What does the term 'whistleblowing' refer to in the context of business ethics?**

    a. Reporting financial performance

    b. Informing stakeholders about organizational misconduct

    c. Conducting market research

    d. Developing corporate strategies

8. **What is a key challenge associated with globalization in business ethics?**

    a. Balancing profit and ethical practices

    b. Finding consensus that meets diverse workforce needs

    c. Managing internal conflicts

    d. Enhancing customer satisfaction

9. **What does the trend of 'Diversity, Equity, and Inclusion' (DEI) focus on?**

   a. Hiring from different economic backgrounds

   b. Promoting only diversity

   c. Ensuring equitable treatment and considering diverse voices

   d. Reducing operational costs

10. **What is a common challenge related to environmental protection in business ethics?**

    a. Decreasing environmental regulations

    b. High costs associated with significant operational changes

    c. Overemphasis on short-term profits

    d. Lack of technological advancements

Answers	1 – a	2 – c	3 – b	4 – c	5 – b
	6 – c	7 – b	8 – b	9 – c	10 – b

Bibliography and References

Chapter 1

1. Brunnermeier, Markus K. "Deciphering the Liquidity and Credit Crunch 2007-2008." *Journal of Economic Perspectives* 23, no. 1 (2009): 77-100. https://doi.org/10.1257/jep.23.1.774o
2. World Commission for Sustainable Development. "Brundtland Commission Report." Accessed July 12, 2024. https://sustainabledevelopment.un.org
3. United Nations. "Sustainable Development Goals (SDGs) (Agenda 2030)." Accessed July 12, 2024. https://sdgs.un.org
4. McKinsey & Company. "A New Look at How Corporations Impact the Economy and Households." Effective 2021. https://www.mckinsey.com
5. Cambridge Dictionary. "Ethics Definition." Accessed July 12, 2024. https://dictionary.cambridge.org
6. Oxford Dictionary. "Ethics Definition." Accessed July 12, 2024. https://www.oxfordreference.com
7. Fayol, Henri. *14 Principles of Management*. Accessed July 12, 2024. https://mmhapu.ac.in
8. Treviño, Linda K., and Katherine A. Nelson. *Managing Business Ethics: Straight Talk About How to Do It Right*. 7th ed. Wiley, 2017.
9. Gert, Bernard. "Morality." In *The Stanford Encyclopedia of Philosophy*. Stanford University, 2005.
10. Rokeach, Milton. *The Nature of Human Values*. Free Press, 1973.
11. Freeman, Edward R., Daniel R. Gilbert, and Edward Hartman. "Values and the Foundations of Strategic Management." *Journal of Business Ethics* 7 (1988): 821-834.

Chapter 2

1. Aristotle. *Nicomachean Ethics*. Accessed July 12, 2024. https://www.academia.edu
2. Kumar, N. S., and U. S. Rao. "Guidelines for Value Based Management in Kautilya›s Arthashastra." *Journal of Business Ethics* 15 (1996): 415-423. https://link.springer.com
3. Prychitko, David L. "Marxism." Accessed July 12, 2024. https://www.econlib.org
4. Drucker, Peter F. "What is Business Ethics?" *The Public Interest* 63, no. 2 (1981): 18-36.
5. Sen, Amartya. "Does Business Ethics Make Economic Sense?" *Business Ethics Quarterly* 3, no. 1 (1993): 45-54. https://www.jstor.org
6. "Mirror Neurons." Accessed July 12, 2024. https://www.ncbi.nlm.nih.gov
7. "Deontology Definition." Accessed July 12, 2024. https://www.etymonline.com
8. "Teleological Ethics." Accessed July 12, 2024. https://www.britannica.com
9. "Duty Ethics." Accessed July 12, 2024. https://www.philosophos.org; https://plato.stanford.edu

10. "Utilitarianism Theory." Accessed July 12, 2024. https://plato.stanford.edu
11. "Virtue Ethics." Accessed July 12, 2024. https://plato.stanford.edu
12. "Ethics of Care." Accessed July 12, 2024. https://plato.stanford.edu
13. NIH BRAIN Initiative. "Neuroethics: Enabling and Enhancing Neuroscience Advances for Society." Accessed July 15, 2024. https://braininitiative.nih.gov/
14. Abend, Gabriel. "Cambridge University Press." Accessed July 20, 2024. https://www.cambridge.org
15. Dembinski, Paul H., Carole Lager, Andrew Cornford, and Jean-Michel Bonvin. *Enron and World Finance: A Case Study in Ethics.* Palgrave Macmillan UK, 2006. https://link.springer.com
16. Ashby, Warren. "Teleology and Deontology in Ethics." *The Journal of Philosophy* 47, no. 26 (1950): 765–73. https://doi.org/10.2307/2020659
17. Barrett, Louise, and S. P. Henzi. "The Social Brain: Evolution and Pathology." In *Evolutionary Cognitive Neuroscience*, edited by S. P. Platek, J. P. Keenan, and T. K. Shackelford, 251-272. MIT Press, 2005.
18. Brierley, B., P. Shaw, and A. S. David. "The Human Amygdala: A Systematic Review and Meta-Analysis of Volumetric Magnetic Resonance Imaging." *Brain Research Brain Research Reviews* 39, no. 1 (2002): 84-105. https://doi.org/10.1016/s0165-0173(02)00160-1

Chapter 3

1. Koontz, Harold, and Cyril O'Donnell. *Principles of Management.* Effective 1968. https://ebrary.net
2. Mintzberg, Henry. *The Nature of Managerial Work.* 1973.
3. Ferrell, O. C., John Fraedrich, and Linda Ferrell. *Business Ethics: Ethical Decision Making and Cases.* Dreamtech Press, 2005.
4. Shaw, William H. *Moral Issues in Business.* 1998.
5. MacKinnon, Barbara. *Ethics: Theory and Contemporary Issues.* 1995.
6. "Tests for Ethical Decision-Making." Accessed July 12, 2024. https://www.ethicsops.com

Chapter 4

1. Harvard Business School Online. "Eye-Opening Corporate Social Responsibility Statistics." Accessed July 12, 2024. https://online.hbs.edu
2. Fordham, A. E., and G. M. Robinson. "Mapping Meanings of Corporate Social Responsibility–An Australian Case Study." International Journal of Corporate Social Responsibility 3 (2018): 1-20.
3. Kotler, Philip, and Nancy Lee. "Best of Breed: When It Comes to Gaining a Market Edge While Supporting a Social Cause, ‹Corporate Social Marketing› Leads the Pack." Social Marketing Quarterly 11, no. 3-4 (2005): 91-103.
4. United Nations Industrial Development Organisation. "What's CSR." Accessed July 12, 2024. https://www.unido.org

5. Bowen, Howard R. Social Responsibilities of the Businessman. 2013.

6. Davis, Keith. "Understanding the Social Responsibility Puzzle." Business Horizons 10, no. 4 (1967): 45-50.

7. Friedman, Milton. "A Friedman Doctrine: The Social Responsibility of Business Is to Increase Its Profits." The New York Times, September 13, 1970. https://www.nytimes.com

8. Freeman, R. Edward, Daniel R. Gilbert, and Edward Hartman. "Values and the Foundations of Strategic Management." Journal of Business Ethics 7 (1988): 821-834.

9. Carroll, Archie B. "A Three-Dimensional Conceptual Model of Corporate Performance." Academy of Management Review 4, no. 4 (1979): 497-505.

10. Carroll, Archie B. "The Pyramid of Corporate Social Responsibility: Toward the Moral Management of Organizational Stakeholders." Business Horizons 34, no. 4 (1991): 39-48.

11. Carroll, Archie B. "Carroll›s Pyramid of CSR: Taking Another Look." International Journal of Corporate Social Responsibility 1 (2016): 1-8.

12. Garg, R., and D. Saluja. "A Business Paradigm for Corporate Shubh–Labh: An Inquest Study." Jindal Journal of Business Research 6, no. 2 (2017): 146-154.

13. Kramer, Mark R., and Michael E. Porter. "Strategy and Society: The Link Between Competitive Advantage and Corporate Social Responsibility." Harvard Business Review 84, no. 12 (2006): 78-92.

14. Kramer, Mark R., and Marc W. Pfitzer. "The Ecosystem of Shared Value." Harvard Business Review 94, no. 10 (2016): 80-89.

15. Kramer, Mark R., and Michael E. Porter. Creating Shared Value. Boston, MA, USA: FSG, 2011.

16. Camilleri, Mark A. "The Integrated Reporting of Financial, Social and Sustainability Capitals: A Critical Review and Appraisal." International Journal of Sustainable Society 9, no. 4 (2017): 311-326.

17. "CSR in India." Accessed July 12, 2024. https://www.india-briefing.com

18. Carroll, Archie B. "A History of Corporate Social Responsibility: Concepts and Practices." In The Oxford Handbook of Corporate Social Responsibility, edited by Andrew Crane, Dirk Matten, Abagail McWilliams, Jeremy Moon, and Donald S. Siegel, 19-46. Oxford University Press, 2008.

19. Mahajan, Ritika. "Corporate Social Responsibility in India: Revisiting Carroll›s Pyramid and the Road Ahead." Pacific Business Review International 7, no. 9 (2015): 91-96.

20. United Nations Industrial Development Organization. "What's CSR." Accessed July 12, 2024. https://www.unido.org/our-focus-advancing-economic-competitiveness-competitive-trade-capacities-and-corporate-responsibility-corporate-social-responsibility-market-integration/what-csr.

21. Porter, Michael E., and Mark R. Kramer. "Strategy and Society: The Link Between Competitive Advantage and Corporate Social Responsibility." Harvard Business Review 84, no. 12 (2006): 78-92.

22. Kramer, Mark R., and Michael E. Porter. Creating Shared Value. Boston, MA, USA: FSG, 2011.

Chapter 5

1. "Brundtland Commission Report." *World Commission for Sustainable Development.* Accessed July 12, 2024. https://sustainabledevelopment.un.org
2. "Sustainable Development Goals (SDGs) (Agenda 2030)." *United Nations.* Accessed July 12, 2024. https://sdgs.un.org
3. Elkington, John. "The Triple Bottom Line." In *Environmental Management: Readings and Cases,* 49-66. 1997.
4. Velenturf, Anne P., and Peter Purnell. "Principles for a Sustainable Circular Economy." *Sustainable Production and Consumption* 27 (2021): 1437-1457.
5. "OPEX Model." Accessed July 12, 2024. https://www.savills.in
6. "Types of Sustainability Reporting." Accessed July 12, 2024. https://eka1.com
7. "Global Reporting Initiative." Accessed July 12, 2024. https://www.globalreporting.org/
8. "Integrated Reporting." Accessed July 12, 2024. https://integratedreporting.ifrs.org
9. "Social Responsibility Report." Accessed July 12, 2024. https://online.hbs.edu
10. "Carbon Disclosure Project." Accessed July 12, 2024. https://www.cdp.net/
11. de Freitas Netto, S.V., M.F.F. Sobral, A.R.B. Ribeiro, and G.R.D.L. Soares. "Concepts and Forms of Greenwashing: A Systematic Review." *Environmental Sciences Europe* 32 (2020): 1-12.
12. "Task Force on Climate-related Financial Disclosures (TCFD) Report." Accessed July 12, 2024. https://www.fsb-tcfd.org/
13. "Sustainability Accounting Standards Board (SASB) Report." Accessed July 12, 2024. https://sasb.ifrs.org/standards/
14. Infante-Amate, Juan, Emiliano Travieso, and Eduardo Aguilera. "Unsustainable Prosperity? Decoupling Wellbeing, Economic Growth, and Greenhouse Gas Emissions over the Past 150 Years." *World Development* 184 (2024): 106754.
15. "Sustainable Development Goals." Accessed July 26, 2024. https://sdgs.un.org/
16. "International Financial Reporting Standards." Accessed July 26, 2024. https://www.ifrs.org/

Chapter 6

1. Sabatier, Paul A. "Top-down and Bottom-up Approaches to Implementation Research." In *Policy Process,* 272-295. Routledge, 2014.
2. Mischell, Walter. *Personality and Assessment.* New York: Wiley, 1968.
3. Watson, John B. "Psychology as the Behaviorist Views It." *Psychological Review* 20, no. 2 (1913): 158-177. https://doi.org/10.1037/h0074428
4. Skinner, B. F. *The Behavior of Organisms: An Experimental Analysis.* New York: Appleton-Century, 1938.
5. Pavlov, Ivan P. *Conditioned Reflexes: An Investigation of the Physiological Activity of the Cerebral Cortex.* Oxford University Press, 1927.
6. Fiedler, Fred E. *A Theory of Leadership Effectiveness.* New York: McGraw-Hill, 1967.

7. Goldberg, Lewis R. "An Alternative ‹Description of Personality›: The Big-Five Factor Structure." *Journal of Personality and Social Psychology* 59, no. 6 (1990): 1216-1229. https://doi.org/10.1037/0022-3514.59.6.1216

8. Costa, Paul T., Jr., and Robert R. McCrae. *Revised NEO Personality Inventory (NEO-PI-R) and NEO Five-Factor Inventory (NEO-FFI) Professional Manual.* Odessa, FL: Psychological Assessment Resources, 1992.

9. MacGregor, James Burns. *Leadership.* New York: Harper & Row, 1978.

10. Bass, Bernard M. *Leadership and Performance Beyond Expectations.* New York: Free Press, 1985.

11. "Sarbanes-Oxley Act." Accessed July 12, 2024. https://www.law.cornell.edu

12. "OECD." Accessed July 12, 2024. https://www.oecd.org

13. "United Nations Principles of Responsible Investment." Accessed July 12, 2024. https://www.unpri.org

14. "UK Corporate Governance Code." Accessed July 20, 2024. https://www.frc.org.uk

Chapter 7

1. "American Marketing Association." Accessed July 12, 2024. https://www.ama.org

2. Pope, Shawn, and Arild Wæraas. "CSR-Washing Is Rare: A Conceptual Framework, Literature Review, and Critique." *Journal of Business Ethics*, no. 137 (2016): 173-193.

3. Calvert, Sandra L. "Children as Consumers: Advertising and Marketing." *The Future of Children* 18, no. 1 (2008): 205-234. https://doi.org/10.1353/foc.0.0001

4. Oates, C., M. Blades, and B. Gunter. "Children›s Understanding of Television Advertising: A Qualitative Approach." *Journal of Marketing Communications* 8, no. 2 (2002): 59-71. https://doi.org/10.1080/13527260210122048

5. "Patagonia Case Study." Accessed July 12, 2024. https://www.mckinsey.com

6. Mazumdar, Prathamesh. "A Study of Business Process: Case Study Approach to PepsiCo." Available at SSRN 2392611 (2014).

7. "McDonald›s Case Study." Accessed July 12, 2024. https://ivypanda.com

8. "Ikea Case Study." Accessed July 12, 2024. https://hbr.org

9. Shen, Bin. "Sustainable Fashion Supply Chain: Lessons from H&M." *Sustainability* 6, no. 9 (2014): 6236-6249.

10. "VUCA." Accessed July 12, 2024. https://hbr.org

11. "Greenpeace." Accessed July 23, 2024. https://www.greenpeace.org

Chapter 8

1. Wood, Stephen. "Human Resource Management and Performance." *International Journal of Management Reviews* 1, no. 4 (1999): 367-413.

2. Greenwood, Michelle R. "Ethics and HRM: A Review and Conceptual Analysis." *Journal of Business Ethics*, no. 36 (2002): 261-278.

3. Hendry, Chris, and Andrew Pettigrew. "The Practice of Strategic Human Resource Management." *Personnel Review* 15, no. 5 (1986): 3-8.

4. Patrick, Parul, and Shabana Mazhar. "Core Functions of Human Resource Management and Its Effectiveness on Organization: A Study." *International Journal of Social Economics* 9, no. 5 (2019): 257-266.

5. Budhwar, Pawan, Ashish Malik, MT Thedushika De Silva, and Praveena Thevisuthan. "Artificial Intelligence–Challenges and Opportunities for International HRM: A Review and Research Agenda." *The International Journal of Human Resource Management* 33, no. 6 (2022): 1065-1097.

6. "Fortune 500." Accessed July 12, 2024. https://fortune.com

7. "Unilever." Accessed June 20, 2024. https://www.unilever.com

8. "Unilever." Accessed June 20, 2024. https://www.unilever.com

Chapter 9

1. Li, Yuhao. "The Case Analysis of the Scandal of Enron." *International Journal of Business and Management* 5, no. 10 (2010): 37.

2. "WorldCom Case Study." Accessed July 12, 2024. https://www.mbaknol.com

3. Wiggins, Rosalind, Thomas Piontek, and Andrew Metrick. "The Lehman Brothers Bankruptcy A: Overview." Yale Program on Financial Stability Case Study (2014).

4. "AIG Case Study." Accessed July 12, 2024. https://insight.kellogg.northwestern.edu

5. Thanos, Lori M. "Tyco International Ltd. Case Study: The Implications of Unethical Behavior." *Academic Leadership Journal in Student Research* 3, no. 1 (2015): 7.

6. Wagner, Stephen, and Lee Dittmar. "The Unexpected Benefits of Sarbanes-Oxley." *Harvard Business Review* 84, no. 4 (2006): 133.

7. Tourish, Dennis, and Naheed Vatcha. "Charismatic Leadership and Corporate Cultism at Enron: The Elimination of Dissent, the Promotion of Conformity and Organizational Collapse." *Leadership* 1, no. 4 (2005): 455-480.

8. "Report of Investigation by The Special Investigative Committee." Accessed July 21, 2024. https://www.sec.gov

9. "AIG." Accessed July 20, 2024. https://insight.kellogg.northwestern.edu

10. "Lehman Brothers 1850-2008." Accessed June 20, 2024. https://www.library.hbs.edu

11. "Tyco International: Leadership Crisis." Accessed June 25, 2024. https://harbert.auburn.edu

Chapter 10

1. "VUCA." Accessed July 12, 2024. https://hbr.org

2. Lamberg, Juha-Antti, Sandra Lubinaitė, Jari Ojala, and Henrikki Tikkanen. "The Curse of Agility: The Nokia Corporation and the Loss of Market Dominance in Mobile Phones, 2003–2013." *Business History* 63, no. 4 (2019): 574-605. https://doi.org

3. "Blockbuster Case Study." Accessed July 12, 2024. https://medium.com

4. "Ikea." Accessed July 20, 2024. https://ikea.com

www.ingramcontent.com/pod-product-compliance
Lightning Source LLC
Chambersburg PA
CBHW070324270326
41926CB00017B/3756